MW00562570

Horst Scheibert

PANZER-GRENADIER MOTORCYCLE & PANZER RECONNAISSANCE UNITS

A HISTORY OF THE GERMAN MOTORIZED UNITS 1935-1945

ORIGINS • ORGANIZATION • EQUIPMENT • OPERATIONS

Schiffer Military History
Atglen, PA

BIBLIOGRAPHY

Erb, Hasso, *Kradschützen*

Fest, Uwe, & Dario, Mike, *Panzerspähwagen* (Band 5 von "Das Waffenarsenal")

Fest, Uwe, & Rieger, Kurt, *Schützenpanzerwagen* (Band 7 von "Das Waffen Arsenal")

Guderian, Heinz, *Erinnerungen eines Soldaten*

Keilig, Wolf, *Das Deutsche Heer 1939-1945*

Müller-Hillebrand, Burkhard, *Das Heer 1939-1945*

Oswald, Werner, *Kraftfahrzeuge und Panzer*

Paul, Wolfgang, *Brennpunkte (6. Panzerdivision)*

Scheibert, Horst, *Deutsche Panzergrenadiere 1939-1945*

Scheibert, Horst, *Schützepanzerwagen 2. Band*

Stahl, Friedrich, *Heereseinteilung 1939*

Traditionsverband der 7. Pz. Div., *Die 7. Panzerdivision im Zweiten Weltkrieg 1939-1945*

PHOTO CREDITS

Bundesarchiv Koblenz (BA)

Generalmajor a.D. Guderian (G)

Schroeder Archives (SCH)

Dr. Hintze (HZ)

Heindorf (HE)

Klippert (K)

Traditionsgemeinschaft der 2nd Panzer Division (2)

Podzun-Pallas-Verlag Archives

Printed in the United States of America.
ISBN: 0-88740-285-2

This book originally published under the title,
Panzer-Grenadiere, Kradschützen und Panzer-Aufklärer,
by Podzun-Pallas Verlag, 6360 Friedberg 3,
ISBN: 0-7909-0177-6.

We are interested in hearing from authors with book ideas on related topics.

Published by Schiffer Publishing Ltd.
77 Lower Valley Road
Atglen, PA 19310
Phone: (610) 593-1777
FAX: (610) 593-2002
E-mail: Schifferbk@aol.com.
Please write for a free catalog.
This book may be purchased from the publisher.
Please include $2.95 postage.
Try your bookstore first.

CONTENTS

INTRODUCTION

The three different service arms described in this book bore the brunt of all major battles the German Wehrmacht fought during the Second World War. Originally motorized, the fighting elements of these arms became partly armored, later on and were used mainly for offensive duties during the early war years, while they were heavily engaged in defensive operations from 1943 to the last days of WWII. Quite often these units had to fight organized into improvised *ad hoc* battlegroups and without connection to their respective divisional units. Serving "fire brigades" duties and being continuously used "to plug the holes" of the cracking front lines, these units suffered severely and finally were destroyed in the maelstrom of continuous action against hopeless odds.

The units described had a considerable edge over ordinary marching field troops as their mobility made them very agile and quick in action, they were safe at least against infantry fire in their APCs, and often they would be supported in action by armored elements of their respective divisions. For all these reasons most of the units described here managed to survived until the end of the war as fighting entities, although all motorcycle units suffered particularly high losses in action. Many of these units had extremely high losses in the Stalingrad pocket and in the Western Desert, and most panzer-grenadiers and motorcycle rifle units, who had already served by the time of the outbreak of war did not live to see its end, while most of the few survivors of the great ordeal have several scars to show to remember these years.

This book is destined to show these arms of service in their entirety, their operational relations and their changes over the war years as well as their cooperation in action, but also the differences between them. A selected collection of photos is added to show the everyday life of those, who lived and fought in fighting and transport vehicles for years on end.

It was a very specific life — full of action, excitement and sufferings — a world, which will remain forever alive and unforgotten by those who experienced it.

The APCs, "soft" transport vehicles, motorcycles and AFVs shown in the photographs are mostly of large scale production variants, but there are also some snapshots of "oddities" and "one off" vehicles.

Horst Scheibert

PANZER-GRENADIER - MOTORCYCLE &
PANZER RECONNAISSANCE UNITS

Although they formed organizationally part of the *Schnelle Truppen* branch, the *Panzer-grenadiere* were a military breed of their own. The forerunners of the panzer-grenadiers — a term officially given to them in 1942 — were the *Schützen* (rifles), the *Kavallerieschützen* (cavalry rifles) and the *Motorisierte Infanterie* (motorized infantry). Together with the *Panzertruppen* (panzer arm), the *Panzerabwehr* (anti-tank defense) and the *Kavallerie* (cavalry) these arms made up the *Schnelle Truppen*, which were created as a separate branch of service in 1938

and were — by then without cavalry forces — redesignated *Panzertruppen* on April 1, 1943. Despite their independent organization, panzer grenadiers and motorcycle rifle units always remained "infantry related", and motorcycle units did not only serve in self contained units, but were to be found within the order of battle of both panzer-grenadier and panzer reconnaissance units as well. So it is easily understandable that after their disbandment in 1943 the bulk of the then still existing motorcycle rifle units were transferred to panzer reconnaissance units.

Here panzer-grenadiers and motorcycle riflemen of the 19th Panzer Division are shown advancing. Central Russian front, 1941.(HZ)

Strictly speaking, the term "panzer-grenadiers" was a misnomer as until the very end of the war the Germans never had enough APCs available to equip even a fair proportion of the panzer grenadier units with armored vehicles. So the bulk of panzer grenadier units had to go into action on soft lorried vehicles of German or foreign origin until 1945.

The creation of the Panzer-grenadier arm came as a direct consequence of Guderian's revolutionary concept or armored mobile warfare. The days of "Infantry, the Queen" were gone and the panzers henceforth were to reign the battlefields, being the supreme weapon upon whose tactical demands all the traditional arms of service had to act. This concept also necessitated the introduction of mobile infantry units, which could accompany the panzers even over difficult terrain into action, safe against infantry fire and shell splinters under the cover of purpose designed armored transport vehicles.

From the very beginning there was a parallel development of the German motorized and armored infantry branch — there was not only lorried infantry, but also motorcycle equipped infantry, the German term for motorcycles being *Krafträder* or *Kräder* in an abbreviated form. Guderian himself explained the reasons for the installation of *Kraftradschützen* (or *Kradshützen* as they were later called) in his book *Achtung, Panzer*, which was first published in 1937. Guderian, then a major general, wrote:

"As we did not have armored transport vehicles with good cross-country performance, those rifle units, which were destined to cooperate with the panzers in action, were instituted partly as *Kraftkradshützen* (motorcycle rifle units) and partly as lorried rifle units, their transport vehicles having good cross-country performance. The *Kradschützen* units, which already had performed well on reconnaissance duties in cooperation with armored cars, can be broken up into tactical sub-units without difficulties, they are very agile and their vehicles can be easily concealed. They can be used on all roads and also over not too difficult terrain. In Germany there are useful motorcycles galore and so there will be no supply difficulties."

Kradschützen remained in frontline service until 1941, but their motorcycles were not well suited to the harsh conditions of the Russian winter and to the quagmires of mud typical for the spring and autumn seasons on the Russian front. These inadequacies combined with the devastating effects of ever increasing fire density on the battlefields, led to a change in equipment in 1942, when the *Kradshützen* had to change their motorcycles for VW-*Kübelwagen* jeeps and amphibious cars and later on, light APCs. As a consequence of these changes there were finally such little differences between panzer-grenadier and motorcycle units, that the latter were completely disbanded in 1943 and the bulk of the still active motorcycle units were transferred to the panzer reconnaissance arm (*Panzer-aufklärungstruppe*).

The *Panzeraufklärungsatruppe* had been equipped with AFVs since its institution in 1935. Obsessed with the tactical concept of "Reconnaissance in force" the *Panzeraufklärer* not only demanded, but were in fact provided with armored cars of different types, Motorcycles, passenger cars, APCs, heavy weapons and even tanks. In consequence, the *Panzeraufklärer* arm developed into a combination of infantry and panzer, not entirely belonging to one of these branches, but in any case suitably equipped for taking the fighting role. Consequently, the tactical use of *Panzeraufklärer* units was not limited to reconnaissance duties, and thus were worn down in innumerable "fire brigade" actions over the war years.

All German panzer and panzer-grenadier divisions had their own complements of panzer-grenadiers, while only the 1st and 23rd Panzer Divisions and some motorized infantry divisions had *Kradschützen* units on strength.

Motorcycles of a *Kradschützenbataillon* (motorcycle rifle battalion) during a rest. The reconnaissance vehicle is a heavy six-wheeled armored car, which was already obsolete by the time of the Western campaign of 1940, when this photo was taken. The letter "G" on the blackout covers of the vehicle searchlights identifies them as belonging to the *Guderian* Panzer Group.

Kriegsgliederung einer Panzer-Division nach dem Stande vom 15. 10. 1935

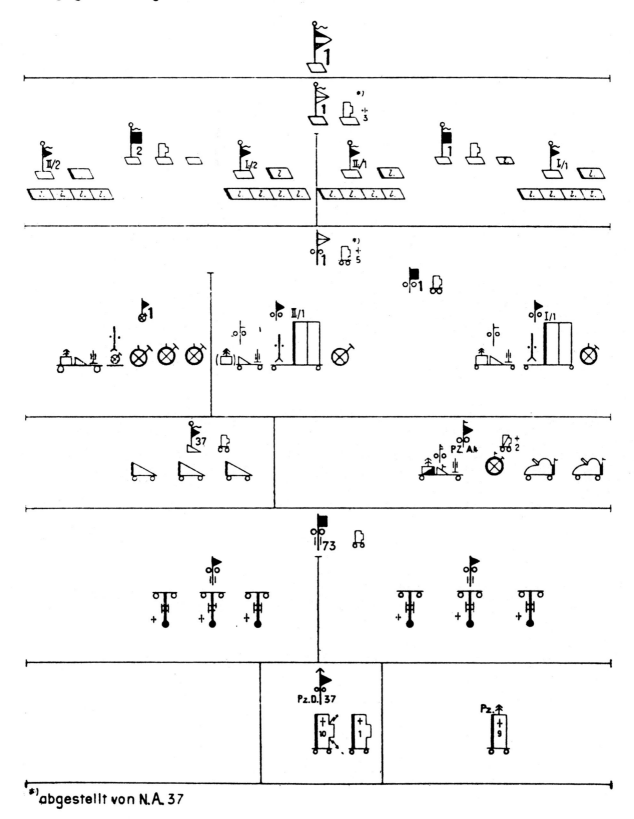

*) abgestellt von N. A. 37

Kriegsgliederung der 1. PANZER=DIVISION nach dem Stand vom 9.5.1940

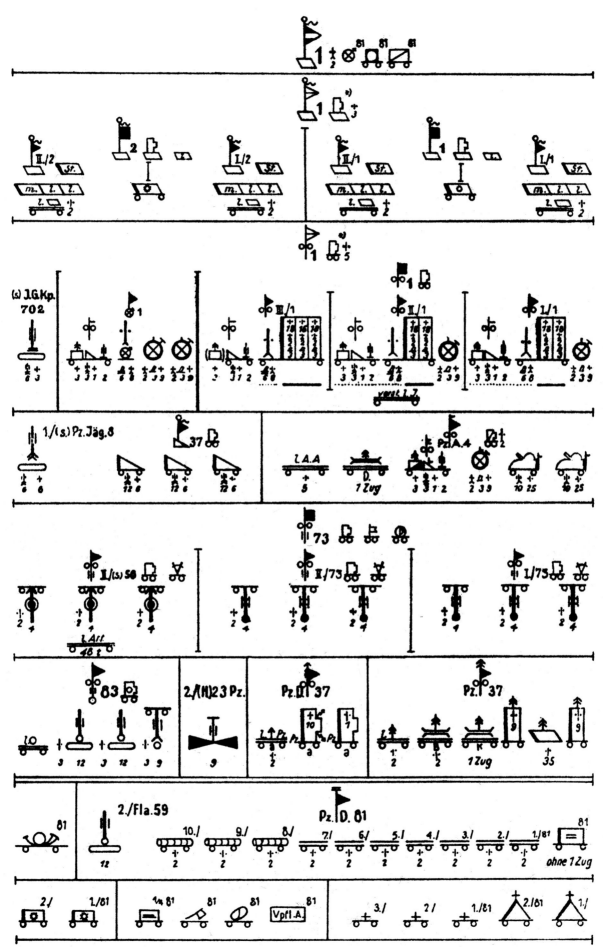

Erläuterung: *) abgestellt von N.A.37   .... = teilweise gepanzert   _____ = voll gepanzert

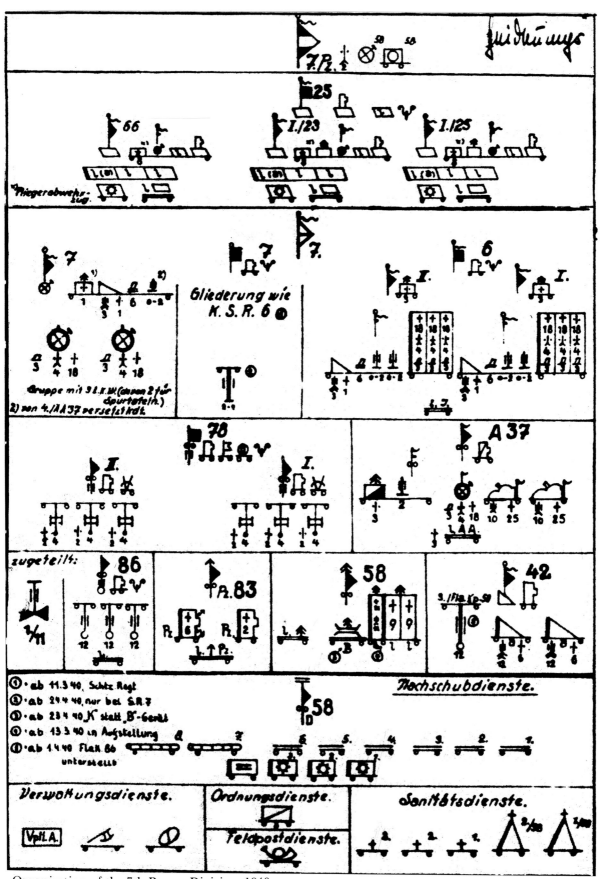

Organization of the 7th Panzer Division, 1940.

Kriegsgliederung 7. Pz. Div. Stand 17.1.43.

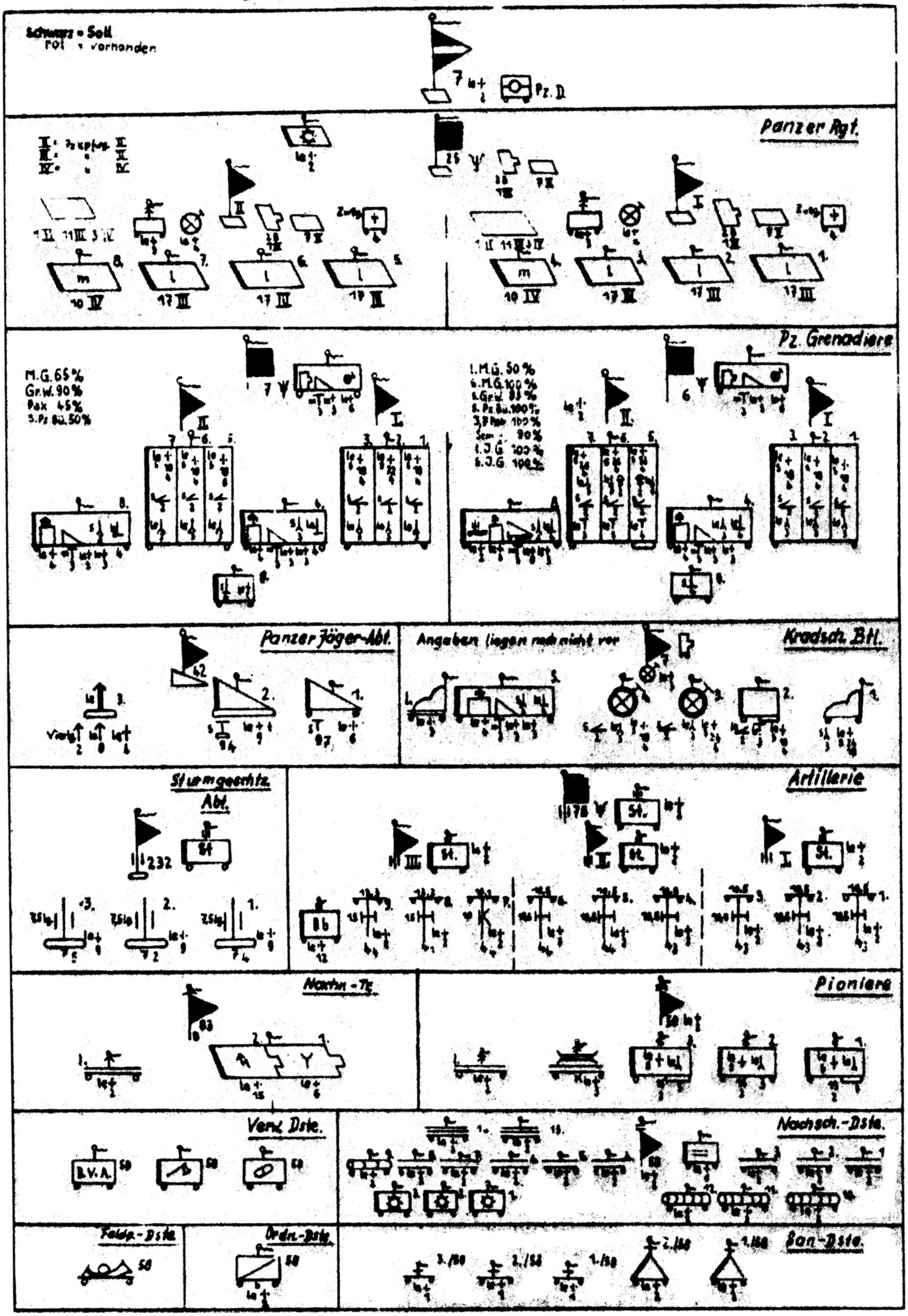

Schwarz = Soll
rot = vorhanden

Panzer Rgt.

Pz. Grenadiere

M.G. 65%
Gr.W. 90%
Pak 45%
3.Pz.Bu. 50%

1.M.G. 50%
6.M.G. 100%
l.Gr.W. 93%
s.Pz.Bü. 100%
3.Pak 100%
Sen. 90%
l.J.G. 100%
s.J.G. 100%

Panzer Jäger-Abt.

Angaben liegen noch nicht vor

Kradsch. Btl.

Sturmgeschtz. Abt.

Artillerie

Nachtn-Tt.

Pioniere

Verw. Dste.

Nachsch.-Dste.

Feldp.-Dste.

Ordn.-Dste.

San.-Dste.

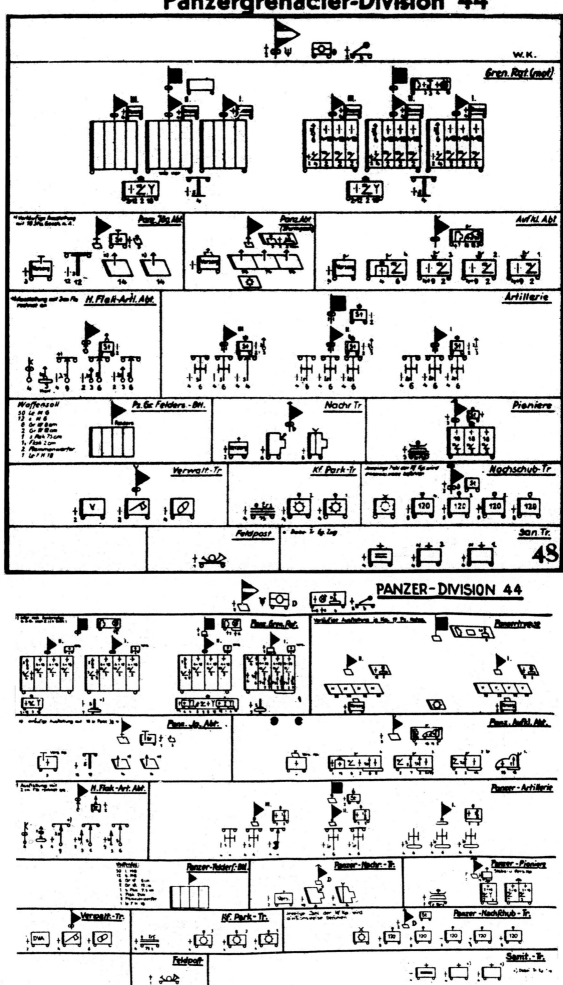

PANZER-DIVISION 44

Only a very limited number of panzer-grenadier divisions were provided *Kradschützen* complements, while *Panzeraufklärer* units were found in all large scale (division etc.) motorized units of the German Wehrmacht. *Panzer aufklärer* were also organized into self contained independent units as *Heerestruppen*.

Organization and relative strengths of panzer-grenadier, panzer reconnaissance and motorcycle elements within panzer and panzer-grenadier divisions varied considerably over the years as can be seen from the organizational tables included on the previous pages (for 1935, 1940, 1943 and 1944 respectively). Besides that, there were also major organizational differences between panzer divisions at any given time as will be found by the comparison between the 1940 order of battle of the 1st and 7th Panzer Divisions.

It will be seen from the above tables that in 1940 the divisional infantry elements — one rifle regiment and one motorcycle battalion — still came under the control of a separate brigade staff. Also, by 1940 the divisional elements of some divisions had been increased to two rifle regiments of two battalions each (see order of battle of the 7th Panzer Division). After 1941 the brigade staff organization was omitted in most divisions, by 1943 brigade staffs were no longer existent and the divisional motorcycle battalions

had been combined with the divisional reconnaissance *Abteilungen*, whereby the newly created units in most cases were designated *Panzeraufklärungsabteilungen*. In several divisions (e.g. 7th Panzer Division) the designation *Kradschützenbataillon* (motorcycle battalion) was retained even after this reorganization. As shown by the sketch even in 1944 only one panzer-grenadier battalion (of four battalions per division) was armored.

In 1935 the average motorcycle battalion was made up of three motorcycle companies, each rifle regiment had two motorcycle companies and each *Panzeraufklärungabteilung* had one motorcycle company on strength. The distinguishing sign of the motorcycle branch was a wheel like four spoked insignia with a stylized steering arm. By 1940 the number of motorcycle companies within the average motorcycle battalion had been reduced to two, while — with a few exceptions (e.g. the 1st panzer division) — there were no more motorcycle elements at all within the rifle regiment. By 1943 "pure-bred" motorcycle battalions had completely disappeared.

Also, within the German panzer reconnaissance units there was a steady decrease of motorcycles over the years, the motorcycles being continuously superseded by increasing numbers of armored reconnaissance cars and

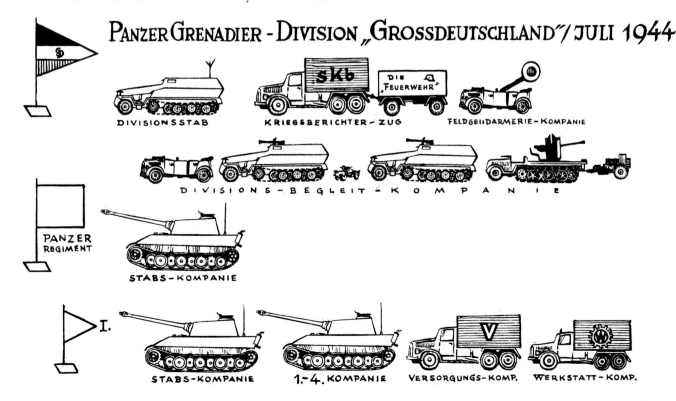

PANZER GRENADIER - DIVISION „GROSSDEUTSCHLAND"/JULI 1944

DIVISIONSSTAB KRIEGSBERICHTER - ZUG FELDGENDARMERIE - KOMPANIE

DIVISIONS - BEGLEIT - KOMPANIE

PANZER REGIMENT

STABS - KOMPANIE

I.

STABS - KOMPANIE 1.-4. KOMPANIE VERSORGUNGS - KOMP. WERKSTATT - KOMP.

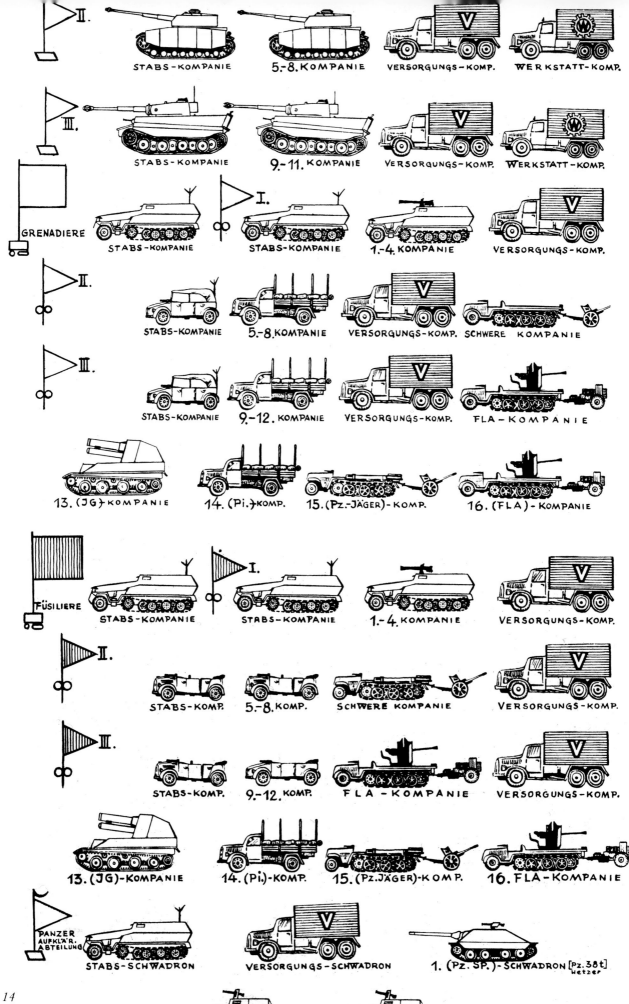

STABS-KOMPANIE   5.-8. KOMPANIE   VERSORGUNGS-KOMP.   WERKSTATT-KOMP.

STABS-KOMPANIE   9.-11. KOMPANIE   VERSORGUNGS-KOMP.   WERKSTATT-KOMP.

GRENADIERE   STABS-KOMPANIE   STABS-KOMPANIE   1.-4. KOMPANIE   VERSORGUNGS-KOMP.

STABS-KOMPANIE   5.-8. KOMPANIE   VERSORGUNGS-KOMP.   SCHWERE KOMPANIE

STABS-KOMPANIE   9.-12. KOMPANIE   VERSORGUNGS-KOMP.   FLA-KOMPANIE

13. (JG) KOMPANIE   14. (Pi.) KOMP.   15. (Pz.-JÄGER)-KOMP.   16. (FLA)-KOMPANIE

FÜSILIERE   STABS-KOMPANIE   STABS-KOMPANIE   1.-4. KOMPANIE   VERSORGUNGS-KOMP.

STABS-KOMP.   5.-8. KOMP.   SCHWERE KOMPANIE   VERSORGUNGS-KOMP.

STABS-KOMP.   9.-12. KOMP.   FLA-KOMPANIE   VERSORGUNGS-KOMP.

13. (JG)-KOMPANIE   14. (Pi.)-KOMP.   15. (Pz.JÄGER)-KOMP.   16. FLA-KOMPANIE

PANZER AUFKLÄR. ABTEILUNG   STABS-SCHWADRON   VERSORGUNGS-SCHWADRON   1. (Pz. SP.)-SCHWADRON [Pz. 38t] Hetzer

2. (SPW)-SCHWADRON

3. (SPW)-SCHWADRON

4. (SCHWERE) SCHWADRON

14

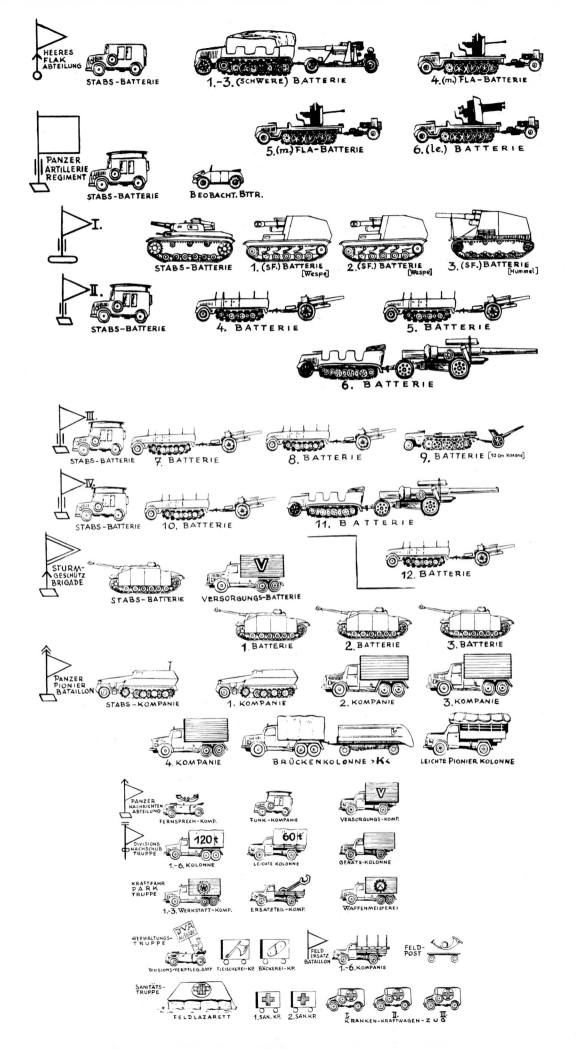

HEERES FLAK ABTEILUNG

STABS-BATTERIE   1.-3. (SCHWERE) BATTERIE   4.(m.) FLA-BATTERIE

5.(m.) FLA-BATTERIE   6.(le.) BATTERIE

PANZER ARTILLERIE REGIMENT

STABS-BATTERIE   BEOBACHT. BTTR.

I.

STABS-BATTERIE   1.(SF.) BATTERIE [Wespe]   2.(SF.) BATTERIE [Wespe]   3.(SF.) BATTERIE [Hummel]

II.

STABS-BATTERIE   4. BATTERIE   5. BATTERIE

6. BATTERIE

III.

STABS-BATTERIE   7. BATTERIE   8. BATTERIE   9. BATTERIE [10 cm Kanone]

IV.

STABS-BATTERIE   10. BATTERIE   11. BATTERIE

12. BATTERIE

STURM-GESCHÜTZ BRIGADE

STABS-BATTERIE   VERSORGUNGS-BATTERIE

1. BATTERIE   2. BATTERIE   3. BATTERIE

PANZER PIONIER BATAILLON

STABS-KOMPANIE   1. KOMPANIE   2. KOMPANIE   3. KOMPANIE

4. KOMPANIE   BRÜCKENKOLONNE >K<   LEICHTE PIONIER KOLONNE

PANZER NACHRICHTEN ABTEILUNG

FERNSPRECH-KOMP.   FUNK-KOMPANIE   VERSORGUNGS-KOMP.

DIVISIONS NACHSCHUB TRUPPE

1.-6. KOLONNE   LEICHTE KOLONNE   GERÄTE-KOLONNE

KRAFTFAHR PARK TRUPPE

1.-3. WERKSTATT-KOMP.   ERSATZTEIL-KOMP.   WAFFENMEISTEREI

VERWALTUNGS-TRUPPE

DIVISIONS-VERPFLEG.-AMT   FLEISCHEREI-KP.   BÄCKEREI-KP.

FELD ERSATZ BATAILLON

1.-6. KOMPANIE   FELD-POST

SANITÄTS-TRUPPE

FELDLAZARETT   1.SAN.KP.   2.SAN.KP.   KRANKEN-KRAFTWAGEN-ZUG

VW *Kübelwagen* jeeps and even light APCs later on. This may be clearly seen from the 1944 organizational table.

The 1944 order of battle of the élite *Grossdeutschland* Panzer-grenadier division is of particular interest as it is also representative for the panzer divisions of the Waffen-SS, and for the Luftwaffe panzer division *Hermann Göring*, which were all similarly organized as the *GD* division.

Only one panzer-grenadier battalion of the divisional panzer-grenadier regiment of each of these divisions was armored, i.e. equipped with medium APCs. While the divisional panzer reconnaissance units were equipped with light APCs, *Kradschützen* elements had been discarded with altogether. By 1944, the separate *Panzerjägerabteilung* of the *GD* division had been disbanded as well, but the division had by then one anti-tank company (designated

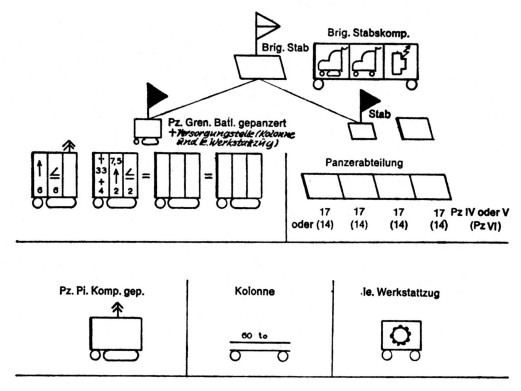

Quelle: Nachr. Blatt des Gen. Insp, der Pz. Truppen von 1944, Nr. 15

Organization of panzer brigades 101 to 113 in 1944. These were independent brigades.

Schwadron in the *GD* and several other divisions), which was equipped with *Hetzer* ("Baiter") hunting tanks.

The following sketch shows the 1944 order of battle for one of the then newly created independent "panzer brigades", which sometimes were also known under the designation "panzer-grenadier brigades." In fact, these brigades were of regimental strength only and comprised one panzer-grenadier battalion (armored) and one *Panzerabteilung* each. Each brigade also had two panzer reconnaissance platoons within its "brigade staff company."

In 1945 there were plans for the institution of "new model" panzer divisions, which should have had included one "mixed" — half panzer-grenadier, half panzer — regiment each. Similarly organized to the "panzer brigade 1944", each of these newly planned panzer divisions was to have only one reconnaissance car equipped *Schwadron* within its *Panzeraufklärungsabteilung*, while it was to have no additional motorcycles and, surprisingly, no APCs on strength.

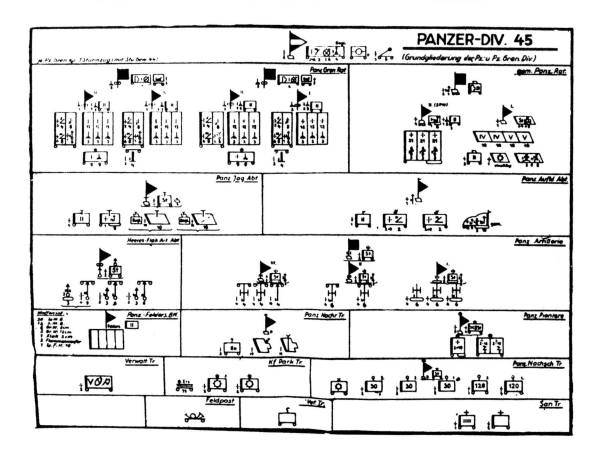

The decision to institute "mixed" (panzer-grenadier/panzer) regiments was the result of practical battlefront experiences gained over the war years. Since 1939, panzer and grenadier (rifle) units had always fought in close co-operation. this fact leading to the development of so called *Coleur-verbände* (coleur-units) within the divisions. The opportunity to create "mixed" regiments had been missed by the outbreak of war and once again in 1941, when the institution of armored panzer-grenadier battalions would have suggested such an innovation even more, the reasons for this high-levelled hesitation being anticipated logistical and training problems, as well as rivalries between the branches of service involved (so for instance the question remained unsolved if "mixed" regiments should come under the control of the panzer or the infantry Inspectorates). The new German *Bundeswehr* faced quite similar problems, for which even the *Heeresstrukturmodell 4* reorganization program of 1980 could not bring any definite solutions, the institution of "mixed fighting battalions" being only a first hesitating step towards the final goal. Although the *Bundeswehr* thus went one step further in the planning or regimental organization than the former Wehrmacht had ever dared to proceed, no perfect solution has been found until now, as each brigade of the *Bundeswehr* is earmarked to have only one "mixed" battalion, the latter to be formed only upon mobilization.

As indicated before, all organizational tables can show sample patterns only, as such not always conforming to reality as a result of well established traditions (i.e. in designations, *Schwadron* in lieu of *Kompanie, Abteilung* in lieu of *Bataillon*), actual battlefront experiences and availability of weapons and equipment. Thus there were always organizational differences not only at the divisional level, but also at battalion or company levels within individual divisions.

Differently to the panzer and "panzerjäger" (anti-tank) branches, the three different branches of service described in this volume soldiered on throughout the war years with the same types of vehicles they had been equipped with in 1939: there were the 4-, 6- and 8-wheeled reconnaissance cars, the medium APC and, later on, the light APC, which continued in production virtually unchanged or with only minor changes and improvements until the end of the war.

17

PANZER-GRENADIERS

The origins of the "panzer-grenadier idea" date back to ancient times. Originally, the only instrument of mobile warfare was the horse. By horse transport warriors could be moved comparatively quickly into action, while the fighting itself was always done dismounted. Later on in history, warriors would use horses not only for transport purposes, but even fought the enemy from horseback. These were the origins for the development of cavalry, on the other hand here also lay the founding principles for the development of war chariots.

While the "cavalry idea" proved excellent not only in theory but under actual battlefield conditions, the war chariot after a period of supremacy around 100 B.C. fell from grace as more men became adept to archery and found that the chariot could be stopped in its tracks by concentrating the fire of arrows against the towing horse rather than against the occupants of the chariot. There were many ideas about developing new types of war carts, but generally speaking such imaginative projects of all kinds did not lead to any practical results on the battlefields. *The drawing opposite is typical for such "war cart ideas."*

Things changed again after the invention of the combustion engine and with the development of motorized vehicles, which could transport soldiers to the battlefields. During the Battle of the Marne soon after the outbreak of World War I, the French improvised large scale manpower transport to battlefront areas by commandeering all taxis and buses available in Paris. This operation, almost legendary by now, may be seen as an early attempt to use motorized infantry in the warfare of our century. While the same is true for some similar German experiments during their last big offensive in the spring of 1918, the real breakthrough of the new concept did not come before the introduction of the tank. The tank was a stable gun platform on a fully tracked chassis, and as such, a means to bring heavy weapons to bear upon the enemy from close quarters even over difficult terrain. This combination of firepower, cross-country ability and armor protection gave the impetus for the development of a new type of infantry unit, which were to be suitably motorized not only to follow the tanks into battle, but also to fight alongside them in concerted action.

In the new German Wehrmacht of the Third Reich, mobile infantry units — the forerunners of the panzer-grenadiers — were known as *Schützen* within the five new panzer divisions, which had been formed before the outbreak of World War II. The motorized infantry elements within the "light divisions" of the Wehrmacht were given the designation of *Kavallerieschützen* and mobile infantry units were also to be incorporated into the then newly designed motorized (mot.) infantry units.

By the outbreak of World War II in 1939, most of the German panzer divisions had one *Schützen* (rifle) regiment each, while the "light division" — although having only one tank battalion on strength — was given either three or four battalions of *Kavallerieschützen* (cavalry rifles) to make up its main attacking force. Each motorized infantry division had three motorized infantry regiments on strength. The distinguishing color of the branch service (*Waffenfarbe*) of peacetime rifle regiments was pink (as with the *Schnelle Truppen*, the panzer arm). A distinguishing feature of the *Schützen* being the letter "S" on their shoulderstraps. The *Waffenfarbe* of the cavalry rifle regiments of the light divisions was yellow (cavalry arm), while the *Waffenfarbe* of motorized infantry regiments within motorized infantry divisions was white (for infantry). After the Polish campaign, when the light divisions were reformed as full panzer

divisions the *kavallerieschützen* received the new designation of *Schützen*, but they kept their traditional yellow *Waffenfarbe* in some instances even until the end of the war.

On July 5, 1942, all motorized and armored infantry units were officially renamed *Panzer-grenadiere*, and received *wiesengrün* (meadow green) as their new *Waffenfarbe*. There were a few exceptions to this rule, some units stemming from former cavalry formations keeping their original yellow *Waffenfarbe*. The regiments of Panzer-grenadier division *Grossdeutschland* also kept the original white color.

Before the outbreak of World War II and still during the Polish campaign, some 95 percent of all German motorized infantry units had to rely upon wheeled transport vehicles only. Motorized infantry units therefore had to fight dismounted, and could not always follow the panzers into action, and so many quick successes gained by

the panzers could not be fully exploited. Very often panzer units would have to fight without their divisional infantry elements, this sometimes leading to unnecessary losses of the tanks in street fighting, in night actions and in difficult terrain.

Thus it was necessary to equip motorized infantry units, with a new breed of vehicles not only suited for road designation of *Mannschafts-tranportwagen* (MTW), later to be changed to *mittlerer (m) Schützenpanzerwagen* transport, but also with sufficient cross-country ability and armor protection to follow the panzers, and to enable the infantry to fight from the mounted position. This concept led to the introduction of an armored half-tracked transport and fighting vehicle with the original ordnance (SPW). The first few vehicles of this new type were delivered to the 1st Panzer Division just in time to be used operationally during the Polish campaign,

Panzer-grenadiers of *Panzer Group 2* (Guderian) advancing during the initial phases of the Russian invasion, 1941.(BA)

where the Sd.Kfz.251 (Special Purpose Vehicle 251) proved to be generally successful, albeit a little underpowered. Despite continued protection, there were never enough medium APCs to satisfy the demands of the several branches of the Wehrmacht. Due to raw material shortages and production difficulties, not even the grenadier units of panzer divisions could be fitted with their full complements of medium APCs, in consequence only one grenadier battalion of an average panzer division could be equipped with such vehicles, i.e. just 25 percent of the infantry strength of the whole division. Thus the bulk of panzer-grenadier units even of panzer divisions had to make do with lorried transport vehicles of German or foreign construction until the end of the war.

Each medium APC was the "home" of a ten man squad of grenadiers. After 1941, all medium APCs came with a moveable machine gun and protective shield on top of the driving compartment. 37mm anti-tank guns were mounted on platoon leaders' vehicles, and during the later war years the medium APC came even as a tank hunter with a long barreled 75mm anti-tank gun. To satisfy ever increasing demands of the other branches of the army, there were also a lot of sub-variants of the APC.

It would be beyond the scope of this volume to describe in depth the different forms and changes of the organization of German panzer-grenadier regiments and battalions. Suffice it to say that there were a lot of changes over the war years caused by practical battle experience as well as by manpower and production problems. All panzer-grenadier units were reformed several times organizationally, and as a consequence of the introduction of new weapons and equipment.

Panzergrenadierregiment (gep.) 1944 (Pz.Div.)

Stab u. St.Kp.

8 Offz.	30 Pist.	9 m.SPW
1 Beamter	104 Gew.	20 Kettenkräder
29 Uffz.	6 MP	7 Pkw (gl.)
106 Mann	9 MP (Bord)	3 Lkw (o.)
5 Hiwi.	5 le.MG	10 Lkw (gl.)
―――	9 le.MG (Bord)	1 Zg.Kw. 8 t
149		

Pz.Gren.Pi.Kp. B

4 Offz.	44 Pist.	14 m.SPW
41 Uffz.	177 Gew.	7 Kettenräder
199 Mann	23 MP	6 Pkw (gl.)
10 Hiwi.	14 MP (Bord)	28 Lkw (gl.)
―――	14 le.MG	
254	14 le.MG (Bord)	
	2 s.MG	
	2 m.Gr.W	
	1 Flak 2 cm	

s.Gesch.Kp.Sf.

3 Offz.	28 Pist.	5 m.SPW
31 Uffz.	92 Gew.	6 Laf. f. s.I.G.
108 Mann	17 MP	5 Kettenkräder
―――	5 MP (Bord)	5 Pkw (gl.)
142	3 le.MG	1 Lkw (o.)
	5 leMG (Bord)	7 Lkw (gl.)
	6 s.I.G.Sf.	9 Maultiere
		9 Anh.
		1 Zg.Kw. 12 t

Pz.Gren.Btl. (gep.) (1 x)

Stab	5 Offz.	9 Pist.	6 m.SPW
	11 Uffz.	24 Gew.	4 Kettenkräder
	27 Mann	4 MP	2 Pkw 6 gl.
	―――	6 MP (Bord)	
	43	6 le.MG (Bord)	

Pz.Gren.Kp. c (gep.) (3 x)

3 Offz.	52 Pist.	23 m.SPW
36 Uffz.	94 Gew.	4 Kettenkräder
151 Mann	21 MP	2 Pkw (gl.)
―――	33 MP (Bord)	
190	18 le.MG	
	12 le.MG (Bord)	
	3 s.MG	
	2 m.Gr.W.	
	7 Flak 2 cm (Bord)	
	27,5 cm K-37 (Bord)	

TE Fhr.s.Kp. (gep.) (1 x)

1 Offz.	3 Pist.	2 m.SPW
8 Uffz.	12 Gew.	3 Kettenkräder
10 Mann	2 MP	2 Pkw (gl.)
―――	2 MP (Bord)	
19	2 le.MG (Bord)	

TE 12 cm Gr.WZg. (gep.) (1 x)

1 Offz.	16 Pist.	7 m.SPW
8 Uffz.	18 Gew.	2 Kettenkräder
38 Mann	6 MP	1 Lkw (gl.)
―――	7 MP (Bord)	
47	7 le.MG (Bord)	
	4 Gr.W. 12 cm	

TE s.Kan.Zg. (7,5 cm) (gep.) (1 x)

1 Offz.	17 Pist.	8 m.SPW
7 Uffz.	4 Gew.	
24 Mann	3 MP	
―――	8 MP (Bord)	
32	2 le.MG (Bord)	
	67,5 cm K-37 (Bord)	

Vers.Kp.Pz.Gren.Btl. (gep.)

4 Offz.	22 Pist.	4 Kettenkräder
3 Beamte	139 Gew.	5 Pkw (gl.)
37 Uffz.	2 MP	4 Lkw (o.)
90 Mann	4 le.MG	31 Lkw (gl.)
29 Hiwi.		5 Maultiere
―――		1 Kr.Kw.
163		2 Anh.
		6 Zg.Kw. 8 t

Pz.Gren.Btl. (mot) (1 x)

Stab	4 Offz.	4 Pist.	4 Kettenkräder
	9 Uffz.	36 Gew.	5 Pkw (gl.)
	29 Mann	2 MP	4 Lkw (gl.)
	―――		
	42		

Pz.Gren.Kp. (mot) (1 x)

3 Offz.	59 Pist.	4 Kettenkräder
29 Uffz.	115 Gew.	11 Pkw (gl.)
165 Mann	18 le.MG	13 Lkw (gl.)
―――	4 s.MG	
197	2 m.Gr.W.	

TE Fhr.s.Kp. (1 x)

1 Offz.	2 Pist.	2 Kettenkräder
7 Uffz.	13 Gew.	3 Pkw (gl.)
10 Mann	3 MP	1 Lkw (gl.)
―――		
18		

TE le.Fla.Zg. (2 cm) (mot. Z)

1 Offz.	14 Pist.	1 Kettenkrad
7 Uffz.	18 Gew.	1 Pkw (gl.)
32 Mann	8 MP	7 Maultiere
―――	6 Flak 2 cm	
40		

TE 12 cm Gr.WZg. (mot. Z)

1 Offz.	8 Pist.	2 Kettenkräder
8 Uffz.	32 Gew.	1 Pkw (gl.)
37 Mann	6 MP	2 Lkw (gl.)
―――	2 le.MG	5 Maultiere
46	4 Gr.W. 12 cm	

Vers.Kp.Pz.Gren.Btl. (mot)

4 Offz.	24 Pist.	4 Kettenkräder
3 Beamte	104 Gew.	7 Pkw (gl.)
30 Uffz.	3 MP	5 Lkw (o.)
71 Mann	4 le.MG	24 Lkw (gl.)
―――		4 Maultiere
108		1 Kr.Kw.
		1 Anh.
		1 Zg.Kw. 8 t

Schützen (motorized infantry) crossing the Polish border on September 1, 1939. The *Krupp-Protzen Kfz. 69* (in the background) were widely used transport vehicles in the motorized battalions of panzer-grenadier and motorized infantry regiments, while the *Stoewer M12* commercial passenger car was a ''rare bird'' in the Wehrmacht inventory.

Krupp-built *Protzkraftwagen* (transport vehicles) of a motorized rifle regiment during a parade. This photo was taken in Vienna shortly after the German occupation of Austria in 1938.(G)

Polish campaign, 1939: transport lorries of a motorized rifle regiment are advancing.(BA)

German infantrymen (rifles, cavalry rifles or soldiers of a motorized infantry unit) catch a ride on a captured transport vehicle. Even during the Western campaign of 1940, when this photo was taken, captured enemy transport vehicles, were pressed into service by the Germans as temporary expedients.(BA)

Infantry (soldiers of a rifle unit or a motorized infantry unit) advancing on a *Protz.Kw* transport vehicle. Used primarily for infantry transportation, these vehicles were used as a means of towing by the other arms of the Wehrmacht as well.(HZ)

Central Russian front, 1941: Motorized riflemen and motorcycle riflemen of the 19th Panzer Division are advancing. The transport vehicles are *Protz.Kw* light prime movers.(HZ)

Lorried infantry elements of the 19th Panzer Division in action. Until the very end of the war the bulk of German panzer-grenadier units had to make do with wheeled transport vehicles.(HZ)

Specially designed to go into action with the panzers, the medium APC Sd.Kfz.251 went into production just before the outbreak of the war. The 1st Panzer Division was the first user of these vehicles during the Polish campaign of 1939. The *Balkenkreuz* national insignias on these half-tracks were uncommon before 1940.(BA)

Possessing only minor differences between them, The "A" and "B" versions of the Sd.Kfz.251 APC featured a two piece frontal armor plate and characteristic frontal bumpers.(BA)

An early version of the medium APC without protective shield for the machine gun. In the background is a platoon leader's vehicle with map platform over the driving compartment.(BA)

Riflemen practice dismounting from a medium APC. As indicated by the machine gun mounting, this 1940 photo shows an early version of the Sd.Kfz.251.(BA)

In the Yugoslav mountains during the Balkan campaign of 1941. The fasciae on the front and protective shield of the frontal machine gun are shown to advantage.(BA)

During a rest in a Greek harbor, 1941.(BA)

Russia, 1941. In the foreground is a medium APC of a regimental staff. In the background are a light "Panzer II" and a 50mm "Pak 38" anti-tank gun. The improvised platform, typical for all command APCs, is of particular interest.(BA)

A company sergeant with captured Russian banner. In the background is the APC of the company commander, easily recognized by the command pennant. Probably for improving the range of fire of the frontal machine gun, the platform has been partly removed.(BA)

For protection under inclement weather, a canvas could be fitted over the open topped crew compartment.(BA)

Western Desert 1942. For identifying this medium APC to friendly aircraft a swastika flag is being carried over the bonnet. Fort Agheila is in the background.(Sch)

Western Desert. As the interior of the Sd.Kfz.251 was rather narrow, most of the personal outfit of the passengers had to be attached to the outside armor plates.(BA)

The "C" version of the Sd.Kfz.251 featured a newly designed single piece frontal armor plate, and distinctive lateral "bulges" of the engine compartment.(BA)

Western Desert. Panzer-grenadiers mounted on a captured enemy "soft" transport vehicle. In North Africa as well as in all other theatres of the war, there were never enough APCs available to the Germans. Most German panzer-grenadiers and motorized infantry units had to rely upon wheeled vehicles for transport.

Panzer-grenadiers in their medium APC. The crew are wearing their steel helmets for impending action. The uncommon camouflage painting is of particular interest.(BA)

Sd.Kfz.251 medium APC in action. This photo was taken in Latvia, 1941.(BA)

Panzer-grenadiers of Panzer-grenadier Regiment 103, which was part of the 14th Panzer Division.(BA)

Central Russian front, 1941. Behind the APC to the right is a captured Russian tank. This photo was taken near Vitebsk.(BA)

Italian front, 1944. As identified by the Red Cross flag, this APC is being used for the transport of casualties. This photo was taken near Nettuno.(BA)

This shot of the interior of an APC of a Waffen-SS unit shows to advantage the bow machine gun, and the protective shield arrangement. There were two further machine guns for crew defense. Canteens and other personal belongings of the crew are all attached to the outer armor plates.(BA)

An "A" or "B" version of the medium APC in action on the Central Russian front, winter 1941-42. The tank is a light "Panzer II."(BA)

This medium APC, *Ausführung* "A" or "B" has lost its front bumper. This vehicle has not received special winter camouflage painting.(BA)

A good shot of the driver seat of a medium APC.

While battle tanks engage the enemy ahead, light "Panzer II" and medium APCs of the 24th Panzer Division are pushing forward on Stalingrad. Ukraine, 1942.(BA)

Vehicles of the 24th Panzer Division negotiating a "Balka" defile. In the foreground is the commander of a "Panzer III." The position of the *Balkenkreuz* sign on the front of the vehicle is rather uncommon.(BA)

Another shot of the same action. The rear machine gun spindle is shown to advantage.(BA)

In the steppe of Southern Russia. A medium APC of the 14th Panzer Division with two captured Russian soldiers. The victory marks on the armor plate show two destroyed enemy aircraft, five armored vehicles and four artillery pieces.(BA)

Panzer-grenadiers in action. Only the steel helmets are seen protruding over the topped superstructure of the APC. Russia, 1942.(BA)

Panzer-grenadiers in an assembly area — waiting for the order to attack.(BA)

Panzer-grenadiers of the 5th Panzer Division riding in an early version of the medium APC.

Panzer-grenadiers of the 10th Panzer Division in action in Tunisia, 1943.(BA)

Southern Russia, 1942. A swastika air identification flag has been fixed over the front MG, which is without its protective shield.

Southern Russia, 1943. A German assault gun in front of a burning house.(BA)

A "C" version vehicle of the medium APC series on guard duties on the coast of southern France. The MG is without its protective shield.(BA)

A "C" version medium APC of the 10th Panzer Division in Tunisia, 1943.(BA)

Living and fighting in the narrow interior of a medium APC over long periods was quite a task, especially under inclement weather conditions.(BA)

Rschev, 1942. After action panzer-grenadiers mount their APCs again.(BA)

Italy, 1944. An impending action is being discussed with panzer officers.(BA)

Central Russian front, 1941. This was the permanent home for a whole squad of panzer-grenadiers.(BA)

PK-Aufnahme: Rothkopf

Helmets off and standing upright — no action is awaited at the moment.

Mined and burned out. Two destroyed medium APCs of the 6th Panzer Division (Rifle Regiment 114).

A medium APC and its crew — an inseparable fighting entity.(Sch)

In 1943 the "D" version of the medium APC went into production. This was the final version of the Sd.Kfz.251, recognizable by its one piece oblique rear armor plate and hinged entrance door. Shown here are vehicles of the 5th SS-Panzer division *Wiking*.(HE)

The improved shape of the hull of the "D" version of the medium APC is clearly shown here. Tactical numbers on APCs were introduced during the later war years.(BA)

The "D" version of the medium APC had a much simplified body shape, the side storage lockers now integrated with the armored hull.(BA)

Panzer-grenadiers of the 12th SS-Panzer division **Hitlerjugend** on exercise in France, 1944.(BA)

While some panzer-grenadiers fight dismounted over rough terrain, their comrades give them support and protection from the APC.(BA)

The entrance door in the rear of the medium APC is clearly shown here.(BA)

The extension on the forward part of the passenger compartment is of particular interest here.(BA)

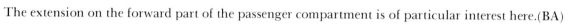

Russia, winter 1943-44. While the tactical numbers have become nearly invisible under the winter camouflage paint, the tactical signs have been carefully masked off.(BA)

Two "D" version medium APCs under improvised camouflage. The platoon leader's vehicle is equipped with a 37mm anti-tank gun.(BA)

Another platoon leader's APC. The 37mm anti-tank gun still has the high protective shield of the original towed version of this gun.(BA)

Two types of gunshields could be found on the 37mm anti-tank gun. This photo shows the later and lower gun shield, which was introduced for improved visibility and retrospectively fitted to many earlier vehicles as well.(BA)

An interesting sub-series of the medium APC was the Sd.Kfz.251/9, which came equipped with a short barreled 75mm L/24 gun.(BA)

This gun-armed version of the medium APC featured thicker side armor for improved crew protection and came mainly with the "D" version of the Sd.Kfz.251.(BA)

The Sd.Kfz.251/16 was a flamethrower version of the medium APC. It was equipped with two 14mm hand operated flamethrowers acting over a distance of more than 60 yards.

Special protective clothing was issued to the crews of flamethrower APCs, but was not always worn in action.(BA)

Exercising again. This photo shows a "D" version vehicle of the medium APC.(BA)

Panzer-grenadier units were equipped with different versions of flamethrower vehicles.(BA)

First issued in 1944, flamethrower APCs did not see much action before the end of the war.

On exercise. These vehicles were primarily intended for extra support duties in street fighting and for action against fortified positions.(BA)

Flamethrower in action. The battlefield is darkened by black clouds of smoke.(BA)

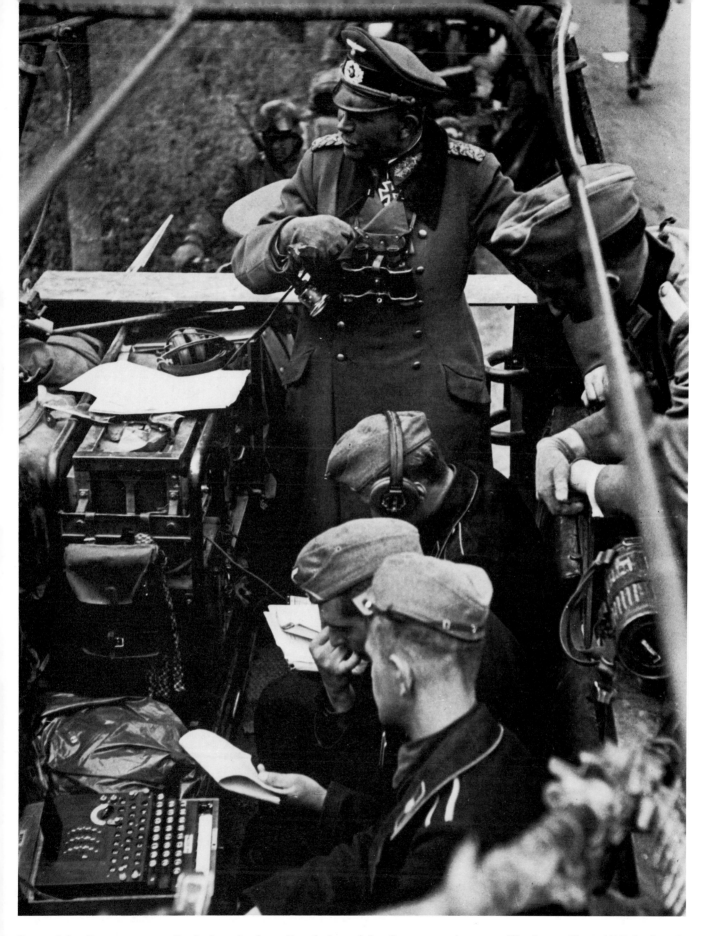

General der Panzertruppen Guderian, the founding father of the German tank arm, utilized a medium APC during the Western campaign in 1940. Guderian was the first commanding general of the Wehrmacht to have an APC redesigned as a "mobile headquarters."(BA)

Guderian discussing further action with *Generalmajor* Kuntzen, commander of the 8th Panzer Division. Western campaign, 1940.(BA)

After 1941, armored command APCs for general staff officers (Sd.Kfz.251/6) could be found in all armored units of the Wehrmacht. Here elements of the 24th Panzer Division are shown pushing forward on Stalingrad, 1942.(BA)

An uncommon construction, probably a field improvisation, is seen here in the Western Desert . . .

. . . but could be found on the Eastern front as well. Shown here is the vehicle of an air liason officer (*Flivo*), in 1942. The *Balkenkreuz* on the front is uncommon.(BA)

Engineer APC mounting bridging equipment. Southern France, 1942.(BA)

An engineer APC less its "assault bridge" outfit. The wooden compartment for extra storage is of particular interest.(B

A limited number of medium APCs mounted three 28cm or 32cm high explosive or jellied-petrol rockets plus launchers on either side of the superstructure. These vehicles ere also known as "Stuka zu Fuss" (Infantry Stukas).

Having an effective range of some 4 kilometers, the blast waves developing after the explosion of theses rockets were of enormous destructive power.(BA)

The Sd.Kfz.251/17 came equipped with a light 20mm "Flak 38" anti-aircraft gun. Shown here is a vehicle of the **Hermann Göring** panzer division of the Luftwaffe.(BA)

Its long 75mm "Pak 40" anti-tank gun gave the Sd.Kfz.251/22 tank hunting capabilities.(BA)

Sometimes "officially", sometimes as mere improvisations medium APCs were used as prime movers as well. This APC is shown towing a heavy 150mm infantry howitzer of the 26th Panzer Division.

Here a 50mm anti-tank gun is being towed by a medium APC of the 24th Panzer Division.(K)

With each passing year of the war, still more youthful faces could be seen in German panzer-grenadier units in ever increasing numbers . . .

. . . soon to become hard bitten by battle experience.

SUMMARY

Unit	Wehrkreis of origin	Division	Notes
Inf.Rgt.(mot) Großdeutschland	III	H.Tr.	erhielt 1940 II./I.R. (mot) 92 als III.Btl.; 1942 Aufteilung in I.R. (mot) GD 1 und GD 2
(Pz)Gren.Rgt.(mot) GD	III	GD	am 1.10.42 aus I.R. (mot)GD 1; wurde 1944 Pz.Gren.Rgt. GD 1
Pz.Gren.Rgt.GD 1	III	GD	
Pz.Gren.Rgt.GD 2	III	GD	aufgestellt 1944
Füs.Rgt.(mot)GD	III	GD	am 1.10.42 aus I.R. (mot) GD 2; wurde 1944 Pz.Füs.Rgt.GD
Pz.Füs.Rgt.GD	III	GD	
(Pz.)Gren.Rgt.(mot) FHH	XX	FHH	FHH = Feldherrnhalle
(Pz.)Füs.Rgt.(mot) FHH	XX	FHH	
Schtz.Rgt. 1	IX	1.Pz.Div.	erhielt 1940 III./I.R. (mot) 69 als III.Btl.
Pz.Gren.Rgt. 1	IX	1.Pz.Div.	aus Schtz.Rgt. 1
Schtz.Rgt. 2	XVII	2.Pz.Div.	erhielt 1940 I./I.R. (mot) 33 als III.Btl.
Pz.Gren.Rgt. 2	XVII	2.Pz.Div.	aus Schtz.Rgt. 2
Schtz.Rgt. 3	III	3.Pz.Div.	erhielt 1940 II./I.R. (mot) 69 als III.Btl.
Pz.Gren.Rgt. 3	III	3.Pz.Div.	aus Schtz.Rgt. 3
Kav.Schtz.Rgt. 4	VI	1.le.Div.	wurde Schtz.Rgt. 4
Schtz.Rgt. 4	VI	6.Pz.Div.	
Pz.Gren.Rgt. 4	VI	6.Pz.Div.	aus Schtz.Rgt. 4
Schtz.Rgt. 5	II	12.Pz.Div.	
Pz.Gren.Rgt. 5	II	12.Pz.Div.	aus Schtz.Rgt. 5
Kav.Schtz.Rgt. 6	IX	2.le.Div.	wurde Schtz.Rgt. 6
Schtz.Rgt. 6	IX	7.Pz.Div.	
Pz.Gren.Rgt. 6	IX	7.Pz.Div.	aus Schtz.Rgt. 6
Kav.Schtz.Rgt. 7	IX	2.le.Div.	wurde Schtz.Rgt. 7
Schtz.Rgt. 7	IX	7.Pz.Div.	
Pz.Gren.Rgt. 7	IX	7.Pz.Div.	aus Schtz.Rgt. 7
Gren.Rgt.(mot) 8	III	3.Pz.Gren. Div.	aus I.R.(mot) 8
Kav.Schtz.Rgt. 8	III	3.le.Div.	nur I und II.Abt.; aus Kav.Schtz.Rgt. 9, I. und II./Kav. Schtz.Rgt. 8
Pz.Gren.Rgt. 8	III	8.Pz.Div.	aus Schtz.Rgt. 8; wurde Pz.Gren.Rgt. 98
Kav.Schtz.Rgt. 9	III	3.le.Div.	trat 1940 mit Stab und I.Abt. zu Schtz.Rgt.8
Pz.Gren.Rgt. 9	III	26.Pz.Div.	
Kav.Schtz.Rgt. 10	XVII	4.le.Div.	wurde Schtz.Rgt. 10
Schtz.Rgt. 10	XVII	9.Pz.Div.	
Pz.Gren.Rgt. 10	XVII	9.Pz.Div.	aus Schtz.Rgt. 10
Kav.Schtz.Rgt. 11	XVII	4.le.Div.	wurde Schtz.Rgt. 11
Schtz.Rgt. 11	XVII	9.Pz.Div.	
Pz.Gren.Rgt. 11	XVII	9.Pz.Div.	
Schtz.Rgt. 12	XIII	4.Pz.Div.	
Pz.Gren.Rgt. 12	XIII	4.Pz.Div.	aus Schtz.Rgt. 12
Schtz.Rgt. 13	VIII	5.Pz.Div.	aus Schtz.Rgt. 13 später Pz.G.R. 13
Schtz.Rgt. 14	VIII	5.Pz.Div.	
Pz.Gren.Rgt. 14	VIII	5.Pz.Div.	aus Schtz.Rgt. 14
Inf.Rgt.(mot) 15	IX	29.Inf.Div. (mot)	
(Pz.)Gren.Rgt. (mot) 15	IX	29.Pz.Gren. Div.	aus I.R.(mot) 15
Gren.Rgt.(mot) 20	XIII	10.Pz.Gren. Div.	aus I.R.(mot) 20
Schtz.Rgt. 21	I	24.Pz.Div.	
Pz.Gren.Rgt. 21	I	24.Pz.Div.	aus Schtz.Rgt. 21
Inf.Rgt.(mot) 25	II	2.Inf.Div. (mot)	wurde Schtz.Rgt. 25
Schtz.Rgt. 25	II	12.Pz.Div.	
Pz.Gren.Rgt. 25	II	12.Pz.Div.	aus Schtz.Rgt. 25
Schtz.Rgt. 26	I	24.Pz.Div.	
Pz.Gren.Rgt. 26	I	24.Pz.Div.	aus Schtz.Rgt. 26
Pz.Gren.Rgt. 28	III	8.Pz.Div.	
(Pz.)Gren.Rgt. (mot) 29	III	3.Pz.Gren. Div.	aus I.R.(mot) 29
Inf.Rgt.(mot) 33	XI	13.Inf.Div. (mot)	
		4.Pz.Div.	wurde Schtz.Rgt. 33
Schtz.Rgt. 33	XIII	4.Pz.Div.	
Pz.Gren.Rgt. 33	XIII	4.Pz.Div.	aus Schtz.Rgt. 33
(Pz.)Gren.Rgt. (mot) 35	V	25.Pz.Gren. Div.	
Schtz.Rgt. 40	VII	17.Pz.Div.	aus I.R.40 (1940)
Pz.Gren.Rgt. 40	VII	17.Pz.Div.	aus Schtz.Rgt. 40
(Pz.)Gren.Rgt. (mot) 41	XIII	10.Pz.Gren. Div.	aus I.R.(mot) 41
(Pz.)Gren.Rgt. (mot) 51	VIII	18.Pz.Gren. Div.	aus I.R.(mot) 51
Schtz.Rgt. 52	IV	18.Pz.Div.	aus I.R.52 (1940)
Pz.Gren.Rgt. 52	IV	18.Pz.Div.	
Schtz.Rgt. 59	XI	20.Pz.Div.	1941 aus I.R. 59
Pz.Gren.Rgt. 59	IX	20.Pz.Div.	aus Schtz.Rgt. 59
(Pz.)Gren.Rgt. (mot) 60	VI	16.Pz.Gren. Div. 116. Pz.Div.	aus I.R.(mot) 60
Schtz.Rgt. 63	VII	17.Pz.Div.	1940 aus I.R. 63
Pz.Gren.Rgt. 63	VII	17.Pz.Div.	
I./Pz.Felders. Rgt. 63	VI	16.Pz.Div.	

Unit		Wehrkreis of origin	Division	Notes
Schtz.Rgt.	64	VI	16.Pz.Div.	aus I.R. 64
Pz.Gren.Rgt.	64	VI	16.Pz.Div.	aus Schtz.Rgt. 64
Inf.Rgt.(mot)	66	XI	13.Inf.Div. (mot)	
Schtz.Rgt.	66	XI	13.Pz.Div.	1941 aus I.R.(mot) 66
Pz.Gren.Rgt.	66	XI	13.Pz.Div.	
Pz.Gren.Rgt.	67	III	26.Pz.Div.	
Inf.Rgt.(mot)	69	X	20.Inf.Div. (mot)	1940 Abgaben von Btl. an Schtz.Rgt. 1 und 3
Schtz.Rgt.	69	X	10.Pz.Div.	Zuführung III./I.R. (mot) 86
Pz.Gren.Rgt.	69	X	10.Pz.Div.	aus Schtz.Rgt. 69
Inf.Rgt.(mot)	71	IX	29.Inf.Div. (mot)	
(Pz.)Gren.Rgt.	71	IX	29.Pz.Gren. Div.	
Schtz.Rgt.	73	XI	19.Pz.Div.	1941 aus I.R. 73
Pz.Gren.Rgt.	73	XI	19.Pz.Div.	aus Schtz.Rgt. 73
Schtz.Rgt.	74	XI	19.Pz.Div.	1941 aus I.R. 74
Pz.Gren.Rgt.	74	XI	19.Pz.Div.	aus Schtz.Rgt. 74
Inf.Rgt.(mot)	76	X	20.Inf.Div. (mot)	
(Pz.)Gren.Rgt.	76	X	20.Pr.Gren. Div.	aus I.R.(mot) 76
Schtz.Rgt.	79	VI	16.Pz.Div.	aus I.R. 79
Pz.Gren.Rgt.	79	VI	16.Pz.Div.	aus Schtz.Rgt. 79
Pz.Füs.Rgt.	79	VI	XXIV.Pz.K.	aus Pz.Gren.Rgt. 79
Inf.Rgt.(mot)	86	X	20.Inf.Div. (mot)	
Schtz.Rgt.	86	X	10.Pz.Div.	III.Btl. wurde 1940 II./Schtz.Rgt. 69
Pz.Gren.Rgt.	86	X	10.Pz.Div.	aus Schtz.Rgt. 86
Inf.Rgt.(mot)	90	X	20.Inf.Div. (mot)	
(Pz.)Gren.Rgt. (mot)	90	X	20.Pz.Gren. Div.	
Inf.Rgt.(mot)	92	II	2.Inf.Div. (mot) 60.Inf.Div. (mot) ab 1941	II. Btl. 1940 aus I.R. GD
(Pz.)Gren.Brig.	92	II	H.Tr. Sonderstab F LXVIII.A.K.z.b.V.	
Inf.Rgt.(mot)	93	XI	13.Inf.Div. (mot)	
Schtz.Rgt.	93	XI	13.Pz.Div.	aus I.R.(mot) 93
Pz.Gren.Rgt.	93	XI	13.Pz.Div.	aus Schtz.Rgt. 93
Pz.Gren.Rgt.	98	III	8.Pz.Div.	aus Pz.Gren.Rgt. 8
Pz.Gren.Rgt.	100	III	Fü.Begleit. Div.	
Schtz.Rgt.	101	IV	18.Pz.Div.	1941 aus I.R. 101
Pz.Gren.Rgt.	101	IV	18.Pz.Div.	aus Schtz.Rgt. 101
Schtz.Rgt.	103	IV	14.Pz.Div.	1940 aus I.R. 103
Pz.Gren.Rgt.	103	IV	14.Pz.Div.	aus Schtz.Rgt. 103
Schtz.Rgt.	104	XII	15.Pz.Div.	zeitw. 21.Pz.Div.
Pz.Gren.Rgt.	104	XII	15.Pz.Gren. Div.	aus Schtz.Rgt. 104 bzw. Rgt. Sizilien 1
Schtz.Rgt.	108	IV	14.Pz.Div.	1940/41 aus I.R. 10
Pz.Gren.Rgt.	108	IV	14.Pz.Div.	aus Schtz.Rgt. 108
Schtz.Rgt.	110	VIII	11.Schtz.Brig. 11.Pz.Div. ab Anfang 1941	
Pz.Gren.Rgt.	110	VIII	11.Pz.Div.	aus Schtz.Rgt. 110
Schtz.Rgt.	111	VIII	11.Schtz.Brig. 11.Pz.Div. ab Anfang 1941	
Pz.Gren.Rgt.	111	VIII	11.Pz.Div.	aus Schtz.Rgt. 111
Schtz.Rgt.	112	IX	20.Pz.Div.	
Pz.Gren.Rgt.	112	IX	20.Pz.Div.	aus Schtz.Rgt. 112
Schtz.Rgt.	113	IX	1.Pz.Div.	
Pz.Gren.Rgt.	113	IX	1.Pz.Div.	aus Schtz.Rgt. 113
Schtz.Rgt.	114	VI	6.Pz.Div.	
Pz.Gren.Rgt.	114	VI	6.Pz.Div.	aus Schtz.Rgt. 114
Schtz.Rgt.	115	XII	15.Pz.Div.	1941 aus I.R. 115
Pz.Gren.Rgt.	115	XII	15.Pz.Div. 15.Pz.Gren. Div.	aus Schtz.Rgt. 115 neu aus Rgt. Sizilien 2
(Pz.)Gren.Rgt. (mot)	119	V	25.Pz.Gren. Div.	aus I.R.(mot) 119
Inf.Rgt.(mot)	120	XX	60.Inf.Div. (mot)	1941 aus I.R. 244; I.R. "Feldherrenhalle"
Füs.Rgt.(mot)	120	XX	60.Inf.Div. (mot)	aus I.R.(mot) 120
Pz.Gren.Rgt.	125	III	21.Pz.Div.	aus I.R.(mot) 125
Pz.Gren.Rgt.	126	V	23.Pz.Div.	
Pz.Gren.Rgt.	128	V	23.Pz.Div.	
Pz.Gren.Rgt.	129	XII	22.Pz.Div. 15.Pz.Gren. Div.	1943 neu aus Rgt. Sizilien 3
Pz.Gren.Rgt.	135		?	Aufstellung fraglich
Pz.Gren.Rgt.	140	XII	22.Pz.Div.	Aufstellung fraglich
Pz.Gren.Rgt.	142	X	Pz.Div. "Holstein" 223.Pz.Div.	
Pz.Gren.Rgt.	146	VI	25.Pz.Div.	
Pz.Gren.Rgt.	147	VI	25.Pz.Div.	
Gren.Rgt.(mot)	148		345.Pz.Gren. Div.	
Gren.Rgt.(mot)	149		386.Pr.Gren. Div.	
Gren.Rgt.(mot)	152		345.Pz.Gren. Div.	
Gren.Rgt.(mot)	153		386.Pz.Gren.Div.	
Schtz.Rgt.	155	III	90.le.Afrika Div.	
Pz.Gren.Rgt.	155	III	90.Pz.Gren. Div.	1943 neu aus Rgt. Sardinien 1
Inf.Rgt.(mot)	156	VI	16.Inf.Div. (mot)	
(Pz.)Gren.Rgt. (mot)	156	VI	16.Pz.Div. 116.Pz.Div.	
Pz.Gren.Rgt.	160		H.Tr.	
Pz.Gren.Rgt.	192	VI	21.Pz.Div. 22.Pz.Div.(?)	
Schtz.Rgt.Stab z.b.V.	200	III	90.le.Afrika Div.	aus Rgt.Stab z.b.V. 200
Pz.Gren.Rgt.	200	III	90.Pz.Gren. Div.	aus Rgt. Sardinien 2
Pz.Gren.Rgt.	264			Aufst. noch ungeklärt
Füs.Rgt.(mot)	271	XX	60.Inf.Div. (mot)	aus I.R. 271
Sond.Vbd. (mot)	287		Sonderstab F (LKVII. A.K.)	verst. I.R. für Nahost-Einsatz; wurde Brig. (mot)
Sond.Vbd. (mot)	288		Pz.Gr. Afrika	verst. I.R.
Pz.Gren.Rgt.	288		H.Tr.	
Pz.Gren.Rgt.	304	XVII	2.Pz.Div.	vorh. Schtz.Rgt.(mot)
Schtz.Rgt.	312		H.Tr.	
Afrika Schtz. Rgt.(mot)	361	III	90.le.Div. (mot)	Bewährungstruppe mit Stab, 2 Btl. zu 5 Kp., I.G.Kp., Fla.Kp., Kol.
Pz.Gren.Rgt.	361	III	90.Pz.Gren. Div.	1943 neu aus Gren. Rgt. 853

Unit	Wehrkreis of origin	Division	Notes
Gren.Rgt.(mot) 382	IV	164.le.Afrika Div.	aus I.R. 382
Pz.Gren.Rgt. 394	III	3.Pz.Div.	1940 aus I./Schtz. Rgt. 69
Inf.Rgt.(mot) 433	IV	164.le.Afrika Div.	aus I.R. 433
Inf.Rgt.(mot) 440	IV	164.le.Afrika Div.	aus I.R. 440
Pz.Gren.Rgt. 492		21.Pz.Div.	Aufstellung 1945(?)
Schtz.Rgt. 565		H.Tr.	aus Feldausb.Rgt. 719
Pz.Gren.Rgt. 890		H.Tr.	von 16. Pz.Div. aufgenommen
Pz.Gren.Rgt. 891		H.Tr.	von 24. Pz.Div. aufgenommen
Lehr-Inf.Rgt. (mot) 900	III	Lehr-Brig. (mot)	
Pz.Gren.Lehr-Rgt. 901	III/ XI	Pz.Lehr-Div.	
Pz.Gren.Lehr-Rgt. 902	III/ XI	Pz.Lehr-Div.	
Gren.Rgt.(mot) 945		345.Pz.Gren. Div.	
Afr.Schtz.Rgt. 961 (tmot)		999.Afr.Brig.	Bewährungstruppe
Afr.Schtz.Rgt. 962 (tmot)		999.Afr.Brig.	Bewährungstruppe
Afr.Schtz.Rgt. 963 (tmot)		999.Afr.Brig.	Bewährungstruppe
Pz.Gren.Rgt. 1027	IV	H.Tr.	
Gren.Brig. (mot) 1027	IV	H.Tr.	von 26.Pz.Div. aufgenommen

Unit	Wehrkreis of origin	Division	Notes
Pz.Gren.Btl. 2101		101.Pz.Brig.	
Pz.Gren.Btl. 2102		102.Pz.Brig.	
Pz.Gren.Btl. 2103		103.Pz.Brig.	
Pz.Gren.Btl. 2104		104.Pz.Brig.	
Pz.Gren.Btl. 2105	VIII	105.Pz.Brig.	
Pz.Gren.Btl. 2106	XX	106.Pz.Brig.	
Pr.Gren.Btl. 2107	V	107.Pz.Brig.	
Pz.Gren.Btl. 2108	XIII	108.Pz.Brig.	
Pz.Gren.Btl. 2109		109.Pr.Brig.	
Pz.Gren.Btl. 2110		110.Pz.Brig.	
Pz.Gren.Btl. 2111	VI	111.Pz.Brig.	
Pz.Gren.Btl. 2112	V	112.Pz.Brig.	
Pz.Gren.Btl. 2113	XIII	113.Pz.Brig.	
Pz.Gren.Btl. 2202		102.Pz.Brig.	
Pz.Gren.Btl. 2206	XX	106.Pz.Brig.	
Jäger-Regiment (mot) "Brandenburg"			1944/45 beim Pz.K. "Großdeutschland"
(Pz.Gren.)Rgt. "Kurfürst"			aus Rgt. "Brandenburg" V; bei Pz.Gren.Div. "Brandenburg"
Pz.Gren.Rgt. "Kurmark"			1945 bei Pz.Div. "Kurmark"
Pz.Gren.Btl. I–III			Führer-Begleit-Brigade (1944/45)
Pz.Gren.Btl. "Reggio"			1945 bei 15. Pz.Gren. Div.
Pz.Gren.Rgt. "Norwegen"			1943 bei Pz.Div. "Norwegen"

Panzer-grenadier units transferred to France for rest and recreation were temporarily fitted with enemy equipment. Shown here is a French "Unit *Kegresse* P107" half-track.(BA)

Grenadiers of the 3rd SS-Panzer division ***Totenkopf*** in action. Until the end of the war some 75 percent of all panzer-grenadier units of the German army (including the formations of the Waffen-SS) could not be equipped with APCs, but had to make do with "soft" lorried vehicles for personnel transport.(BA)

MOTORCYCLE UNITS

Motorcycle rifle units were first formed in 1935 not only because the German motorcycle industry, one of the most predominant in the world, could supply a substantial number of these vehicles for military use, but also for the excellent mobility which could be expected from motorcycle equipped units. For infantry motorization purposes, the Germans could only rely on wheeled *Protz* transport vehicles and custom built lorries, which offered less mobility and speed in action then motorcycles. Mounting and dismounting could be very quickly effected by motorcycle riflemen, and on of their operational advantages was their excellent speed in pursuing retreating enemy forces.

Kradschützenabteilungen were incorporated not only into the strength of a few *Kavallerieschützenregimenter* (cavalry rifle regiments) and *Aufklärungsregimenter* (mot - motorized reconnaissance regiments), but also by October 15, 1935 the 2nd and 3rd Panzer Divisions had one *Kradschützenbataillon* each. *Kradschützen* units served within *Schützen* battalions and motorized reconnaissance battalions, and in 1937 an independent motorcycle rifle battalion was added to the then new 1st "light division" of the Wehrmacht.

Being in widespread use throughout the army (Heer), the *Kradschützen* since 1938 organizationally formed part of the *Schnelle Truppen*

The 2nd Motorcycle Battalion of the 2nd Panzer Division parading in Vienna. After the occupation of Austria, a combined parade of the former Austrian "Bundesheer" (Austrian Federal Army) and the German Wehrmacht was held before Hitler on March 15, 1938.(G)

branch and — in common with German tank unit — were to have the white *Waffen farbe* (service color). Only those motorcycle units, which were not incorporated into the order of battle in the first three panzer divisions or of rifle battalions either, did retain their traditional golden yellow cavalry service color. Independent battalions sported the letter "K" on their shoulderstraps.

Before the beginning of the Western Campaign in 1940, most motorized reconnaissance regiments were disbanded, their motorcycle elements being reformed as independent motorcycle battalions with the new service color *Wiesengrün* (meadow green). Although there were some exceptions to this rule, most *Abteilungen* were redesignated *Bataillone* and their respective sub-units were no longer called *Schwadrone*, but simply *Kompanien*. Quite a few units disliked the new designation *Kompanie* and for some time clung to their old designation *Schwadrone*.

During the Western Campaign there were three different types of motorcycle battalions with the following organization:

Type A (1st and 3rd Panzer Divisions):

Headquarters (including signals platoon and light column)

Two of three motorcycle companies, each equipped with 9 light and 2 heavy machine guns plus 3 mortars

One heavy motorcycle company (including one engineer, light infantry howitzer and anti-tank platoon)

Type B (6th and 8th Panzer Divisions):

Headquarters (organized as above)

Three motorcycle companies with 18 light and 2 heavy machine guns plus 3 light mortars each

One heavy motorcycle company with 8 heavy machine guns, 6 medium mortars and 3 anti-tank guns

Type C (7th Panzer Division):

Headquarters (organized as above)

Two motorcycle companies with 18 light and 4 heavy machine guns, plus 3 light mortars each

In the 9th Panzer Division the *Kradschützen* formed part of the divisional reconnaissance

regiment. Designated the *1. Abteilung* of this regiment, the *Kradschützen* elements were organized as follows:

Headquarters (organized as above)

Three motorcycle *Schwadrone* with 18 light and 4 heavy machine guns plus 3 light mortars each

One heavy motorcycle *Schwadrone* with 6 medium mortars, 4 light infantry howitzers, 3 anti-tank guns, plus one motorcycle engineer platoon

The motorcycle combinations of these units were mainly produced by the firms of BMW, Zündapp, Viktoria and NSU. There were different types of motorcycles, but as a common feature most models came with two cylinder opposite stroke engines about 750cc and offering 18 to 26 hp. After 1942 several *Kradschützen* units were issued VW *Kübelwagen* and amphibious jeeps (*Schwimmwagen*). A few companies were even equipped with light APCs of the Sd.Kfz.250 type. Also in use by *Kradschützen* were NSU built *Kettenkräder* 1/2- ton three-quarter tracked prime movers. As a consequence of this reorganization and steady issue of new equipment, there were finally such little differences between *Panzergrenadier* and *Kradschützen* units that the latter were formally disbanded on March 24, 1943 never to be reformed again.

A photo from the institution of the 2nd Motorcycle Rifle Battalion in Bad Kissingen, 1937.(2)

Thus the once uniquely multi-faceted shape of the German infantry arm was finally lost at the end of a development, which for the *Krad-schützen* branch had begun with the changeover from motorcycles to other transport vehicles. What remained afterwards, was a certain melancholy not only felt by the once proud motorcycle rifle branch, but also by all who had witnessed their brave actions. Gone was the old cavalry pride, which the *Kradschützen* had inherited to a far larger extent than the less cavalry-related panzer arm. Like those, who in our days may enjoy the excitement of a ride on their "hot wheels", the motorcycle riflemen of

the German army always had felt to be "something special" and their performances on maneuvers, "Day of the Wehrmacht" shows or party rallies had always attracted the attention of emphatic spectators. Under real battle conditions the breathtaking action gimmicks of the *Kradschützen* —advancing and dismounting at seemingly full speed — could not be repeated, as in most cases attacks has to be carried over lesser known terrain. Having lost their pre-war glamour, *Kradschützen* would normally fight in the tactical role of motorized infantry after dismounting.

Motorcycle riflemen of the 24th Panzer Reconnaissance Battalion (24th Panzer Division) in action on the southern Russian front, late summer 1942.(BA)

Motorcycle rifle unit of the 3rd Panzer Division passing through the Brandenburg Gate, Berlin 1936.

84

Elements of the "Motorcycle rifle battalion" of an improvised *ad hoc* panzer division on exercises in the Lüneburger Heide, September 1935.(BA)

Another shot of the 1938 parade in Vienna.(G)

Dismounting from rolling motorcycles — just a gimmick for parade purposes.(BA)

Motorcycle and reconnaissance cars passing through a destroyed Polish town, 1939.

Another action shot from the Polish campaign. The tactical signs identify a rifle unit.(BA)

Motorcycle riflemen of a reconnaissance unit (identified by the tactical insignia on the mudguard) on exercise before the campaign in the West.(BA)

Fording shallow rivers offered no problems.(BA)

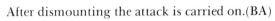

After dismounting the attack is carried on.(BA)

There were to be no delays while mounting the vehicles.(BA)

Cross-country attack.(BA)

Amassing vehicles in such a very tight formation was only possible under conditions of ones own air supremacy.(BA)

Motorcycle riflemen of a reconnaissance unit during the French campaign, 1940.(BA)

A motorcycle reconnaissance party of the staff of a rifle regiment. The "G" identifies vehicles of the *Guderian* Panzer Group.(BA)

A motorcycle combination of the 38th Engineer Battalion belonging to the 2nd Panzer Division during the Western campaign, 1940.(BA)

Favorite "duty" — taking lunch, France 1940.(BA)

Motorcycle riflemen of the 5th Panzer Division during the Balkan campaign, 1941.(BA)

An improvised bypass — Balkan campaign towards the end of April, 1941.(BA)

German motorcycle riflemen in Greece.(BA)

A company of motorcycle riflemen advancing into Russia, 1941.(BA)

Lithuania, 1941. In the foreground are some motorcycle riflemen of the 6th Panzer Division. In the background are ex-Czechoslovakian battle tanks of the 35(t) type.(BA)

Motorcycle riflemen of the 7th Panzer Division in Russia. Vehicles of *Panzergruppe 2* were identified by the capital letter "G" (after *Generaloberst* Guderian).(BA)

Motorcycle combination of a "propaganda company" (see "PK" on the searchlight) of *Panzergruppe 1* (see "K" on the mudguard). The emblem of this particular unit was a wild duck on a tank (see front of the pillion).(BA)

In Eastern Poland, which had been temporarily occupied by the Red Army during the Polish campaign of 1939, motorcycle riflemen of the 12th Panzer Division are hailed as liberators. The year is 1941.(BA)

During a halt in a Russian village, summer 1941.(BA)

Motorcycle riflemen of the 8th Panzer Division.(BA)

Motorcycle riflemen of the 6th Panzer Division in action between Lake Peipus and Leningrad, 1941.(BA)

Elements of a battle group of the 1st Panzer Division. The motorcycles are followed up by the medium and light APCs and a complement of panzers. The prime movers are one ton half-tracks.(BA)

Motorcycle riflemen of 19th Motorcycle Rifle Battalion in 1942. This striking shot speaks for itself.(HZ)

Motorcycle riflemen were in action in the Western Desert as well, albeit the only complete unit to be used in this theatre of operations was the 15th Motorcycle Battalion of the 15th Panzer Division.(BA)

There were also motorcycle elements within divisional reconnaissance units.(BA)

Motorcycle riflemen of the 12th Panzer Division in Russia, 1941.(BA)

Dzisma, March 9, 1941: Motorcycle riflemen of the 19th Panzer Division are preparing for further advance.(HZ)

A "tense" situation. The machine-gunner is ready to commence firing.(BA)

A reconnaissance party of a battalion of panzer-grenadiers from the *Grossdeutschland* Regiment on the Eastern front, 1942.(BA)

Negotiating difficult terrain meant "action as always."(BA)

Action! After dismounting, the motorcycles are brought into cover — Eastern front, July 1941.(BA)

The motorcycle battalion of the 1st SS-Panzer division *Leibstandarte Adolf Hitler*, Russia 1941.(BA)

Motorcycle riflemen of the **Hermann Göring** Panzer Division.(BA)

German paratroop divisions had motorcycle rifle elements as well, though not organized into separate units.(BA)

Elements of the **LAH** Waffen-SS division advancing towards Kharkov, March 1943.(BA)

Some sort of fun (true artists even completed this performance by dismounting and re-mounting the wheel of the pillion during the "show").(BA)

Even after changing their motorcycles for other vehicles (mainly VW-*Kübelwagen* jeeps), the original tactical signs of motorcycle rifle units remained unchanged.(BA)

The motorcycle rifle battalion of the motorized infantry division **Grossdeutschland** had five "squadrons" (i.e. companies): the first company equipped with reconnaissance tanks, the second company light APCs, while the third and fourth had VW-*Kübelwagen* passenger cars (see photo). The fifth ("heavy") company had a strong complement of anti-tank guns.(BA)

A Waffen-SS unit on parade in Paris. Put into large scale production in 1942, the VW-*Schwimmwagen* amphibious jeeps were primarily delivered to motorcycle units.(BA)

Amphibious VW-*Schwimmwagen* in action with the 2nd SS-Panzer division **Das Reich** on the Eastern front in 1943. In the background are *Panther* battle tanks and medium APCs.(HE)

This armored staff car of the motorcycle battalion of the *Grossdeutschland* motorized division is leading a column of light APCs of the 2nd company of the battalion.(BA)

Another action shot of the light APCs of the 2nd company, of the motorcycle battalion of the *Grossdeutschland* division.(BA)

Light APCs of the 10th Panzer Division. After 1942, many motorcycle units became equipped with light APCs in place of the original motorcycles.(BA)

The interiors of these vehicles were all but spacious.(BA)

As the carrying capacity of the light APC was very limited, it was not ideally suited to battle duties.(BA)

Four holders of the *Knight's Cross* (to the left is Major Quentin, OC of Pz.A.A. 6 of the 6th Panzer Division).

There were many sub-versions of the light APC as well. Shown here is a Sd.Kfz.250/5 light artillery observation vehicle of the 7th Panzer Division.(BA)

This sub-version came equipped with the 28mm s.PzB, a 28/20mm tapered bore anti-tank gun, and one machine gun.(BA)

Similar to the Sd.Kfz.251/10, the Sd.Kfz.250/10 was equipped with a light 37mm anti-tank gun.(BA)

The square extra compartment fixed to the back of the vehicle (above left) identified another artillery sub-version of the Sd.Kfz.250.(BA)

The Sd.Kfz.250/3 was a radio command vehicle, of which type there were four sub-versions in the light APC series.(BA)

Rommel's light Sd.Kfz.250. It had the inscription *Greif* ("Griffon") painted on either side of the superstructure, and was famous throughout the entire ***Afrikakorps***. In this photo only the letter "G" is visible.(BA)

Shown here is a light ammunition carrier Sd.Kfz.252 vehicle, another sub-version of the light APC series. Introduced in 1942, the ammo carrier is standing here alongside a medium battle tank "Panzer IV" of the 10th Panzer Division — Tunisia, 1942.(BA)

The uncommon shape of the rear body layout identifies another sub-version of the light APC.(BA)

The Sd.Kfz.250/9 came with a 20mm KwK 38L/55 mounted in an open topped rotating turret. Though used for reconnaissance duties, this photo shows a vehicle captured by U.S, forces and used against its former owners.(Sch)

The NSU produced *Kettenkrad* was in fact a light prime mover in use by all arms of the Wehrmacht. Here it is seen serving with the 2nd Fallschirmjäger Division in Tunisia, 1943.(BA)

As a half-ton prime mover, the official designation of this vehicle as a "tracked motorcycle" (*Kettenkrad*) was misleading.

The *Kettenkrad* was ideally suited to negotiating muddy and otherwise difficult terrain, and was therefore used by field commanders for short distance cross country inspection tours as well.(BA)

Cable-laying was one of the duties in which the *Kettenkrad* performed excellently.(BA)

. . . however, it was not exclusively used as a prime mover.

Put into full scale production in 1942, a grand total of 8345 *Kettenkräder* were completed before the end of the war.(BA)

SUMMARY

Unit	Wehrkreis of origin	Division	Notes
1	IX	1.Pz.Div.	
2	XVII	2.Pz.Div.	
3	III	3.Pz.Div.	
bt. 4	I	1.Kav.Div.	aus Radf.Abt. 1; sp.Pz. A.A.
6	VI	1.le.Div.	aus IV./Kav.Schtz.R.4 24
		6.Pz.Div.	
7	IX	7.Pz.Div.	aus Aufkl.Rgt.(mot) 7
8	III	8.Pz.Div.	aus II./Kav.Schtz.Rgt. 9
10	V	10.Pz.Div.	
15	XII	15.Pz.Div.	
16	VI	16.Pz.Div.	aus M.G.Btl.(mot) 1
17	VII	17.Pz.Div.	aus I.R. 41 und II./I.R. 63
18	IV	18.Pz.Div.	
19	XI	19.Pz.Div.	
20	IX	20.Pz.Div.	aus III./I.R. 115
22	II	12.Pz.Div.	
23	V	23.Pz.Div.	wurde Pz.A.A. 8
24	XII	22.Pz.Div.	wurde Pz.A.A. 5
25	V	25.Inf.Div. (mot)	
29	IX	29.Inf.Div. (mot)	
30	X	20.Inf.Div. (mot)	aus III./I.R. 25
34	XIII	4.Pz.Div.	
36	XII	36.Inf.Div. (mot)	
38	VIII	18.Inf.Div. (mot)	siehe auch A.A. 18 (mot)
40	XIII	10.Inf.Div. (mot)	aus M.G.Btl. 6; sp. Pz.A.A. 110
43	XI	13.Pz.Div.	
53	III	3.Inf.Div. (mot)	
54	IV	14.Inf.Div. (mot)	
Kp. 54	VII	1.Geb.Div.	zeitweise
55	VIII	5.Pz.Div.	
59	XVII	9.Pz.Div.	1941 aus I./Aufkl.Rgt.9
61	VIII	11.Pz.Div.	
64	IV	14.Pz.Div.	1940 aus 3./I.R. 10, 5. u. 9./I.R. 52 1. u. 2./M.G.Btl. 7
160	XX	60.Inf.Div. (mot)	
165	VI	16.Inf.Div. (mot)	wurde Pz.A.A. 116
345		345.Pz.Gren. Div.	wurde A.A. 345 (mot)
Lehr-Btl. 386	H.Tr.	386.Pz.Gren. Div.	wurde A.A. 386 (mot)
"Großdeutschland"		Pz.Gren. "Großdeutschland"	wurde Pz.A.A. "GD"

PANZER RECONNAISSANCE UNITS

It was self-evident that the reconnaissance elements of the then fledgling panzer divisions of the German Wehrmacht had to be armored as well. Similar to the panzer and motorcycle units of the Wehrmacht, also the armored reconnaissance units had their organizational origin in the *Kraftfahrabteilung 6* which was posted in Münster since 1929. Contrary to the panzergrenadiers, who represented a completely new military branch by the time of their constitution,

Armored cars of the 2nd Panzer Division (then forming part of the *Guderian* Panzer Group) during the Western campaign of 1940. A light 4-wheeled armored car (Sd.Kfz.221) is shown here being followed up by a heavy six-wheeler, a Sd.Kfz.232 radio armored car.(BA)

the armored reconnaissance units had fore-runners: armored wheeled vehicles had been used operationally during World War I and developments in this field had continued steadily also during the inter-war years. This led to the introduction of four- and six-wheeled armored cars, the latter to be superseded by eight-wheeled reconnaissance vehicles during World War II.

Even before the institution of the first independent battalions within the first three panzer divisions of the new Wehrmacht, motorized reconnaissance units had been partly equipped with *Kradschützen* (motorcycle) elements organized into single *Schwadrone* or even complete *Abteilungen* within motorized reconnaissance regiments. Seen from this point of view, this arm acted as a sort of "foster-mother" for the then fledgling *Kradschützen*.

Hence the so-called *Schnelle Abteilungen (Mot.)* organizationally did not form part of the armored reconnaissance arm, they will not be dealt with here in any detail. Mostly being *ad hoc* improvisations in the field, and simply "children of war" they would normally be just ordinary motorized infantry units, which served extra reconnaissance duties within ordinary infantry divisions or at corps level.

By the outbreak of war in 1939, the motorized reconnaissance elements within the *Schnelle Truppen* branch were organized as follows: The 1st to 5th Panzer Divisions, the 1st "Light Division" and the 1st Cavalry Brigade had one motorized *Aufklärungsaufteilung* each. Each *Abteilung* consisted of:

Headquarters (including signals platoon)
Two armored car *Schwadrone* (with 4-, 6- and 8-wheelers)
One motorcycle *Schwadrone* (equipped with motorcycles)
One heavy *Schwadrone* (for anti-tank duties etc.)
One "light column" (for transportation)

The 2nd, 3rd and 4th Light Divisions had one motorized reconnaissance regiment each. This regiment was organized as follows:

Headquarters and two *Abteilung* (i.e batalions), each *Abteilung* consisting of three or four motorcycle or armored car *Schwadrone* (of company strength each)

The 2nd and 4th Light Divisions had one reconnaissance *Abteilung* each

The 2nd, 13th, 20th and 29th motorized infantry divisions had one reconnaissance *Abteilung* each. The organization of each *Abteilung* was as follows:

Headquarters and signals platoon
One motorcycle *Schwadrone*
One armored car *Schwadrone*

Within the *Heeretruppen* (independent units) there was an extra and self-contained *Aufklärungslehr-Abteilung* (battalion) which was similarly organized to the motorized *Aufklärungsabteilungen* of panzer divisions.

In common with other branches of the German army, the motorized *Aufklärungs-truppe* underwent a series of modifications and reorganizations during the war years:

1939-40	The reconnaissance regiments of the 2nd to 4th Light Divisions were organized into self-contained motorized *Aufklärungs-abteilungen* and motorcycle battalions
1940-41	The motorized infantry divisions were equipped with motorcycle battalions and a third (heavy) *Schwadron* was added to the *Aufklärungsabteilung* of each of these divisions
1941-42	There were further measures for the organizational unification of the motorized *Aufklärungsabteilung*
1943	The then still existing motorcycle battalions were combined with the motorized *Aufklärungsabteilungen* of their respective divisions to form newly organized *Panzeraufklärungs-abteilungen*. During this process there were some changes to the then existing numerical system as well. No longer forming part of the *Schnelle Truppen* branch, but forming part of the *Panzer-truppen* now, the tactical reconnaissance units were renamed *Kompanien*

An eight-wheeled heavy radio armored car (*Panzerspähwagen*) during the Balkan campaign, 1941. Like its predecessor, the heavy six-wheeled radio armored car, this type of eight-wheeler had the official designation Sd.Kfz.232.(BA)

in place of their former designation *Schwadrone*. In fact there were some exceptions to this rule, e.g. with the *Grossdeutschland* division.

After 1943 *Panzeraufklärungsabteilungen* would be made up of the following sub-units:

Panzerspähkompanie (equipped with armored reconnaissance units)

Panzeraufklärungskompanie (formerly: motorcycle company)

Panzeraufklärungskompanie (equipped with *Kübelwagen*-jeeps)

Panzeraufklärungskompanie (gep) (equipped with light APCs)

Schwere Panzeraufklärungskompanie consisting of:

80mm mortar platoon (motorized or armored) light anti-aircraft platoon (20mm a/a guns)

Light a/a platoon (MG 151 Machine guns on triple mountings for a/a duties)

S c h w i m m - P a n z e r s p ä h w a g e n z u g (amphibious reconnaissance car platoon

Panzerspähwagen-Werkstattzug (reconnaissance repair platoon)

With the exception of those reconnaissance units that were integrated into the first five panzer divisions (service color: pink), all reconnaissance units were identified by the golden yellow *Waffenfarbe* of the cavalry and by the letter "A" on the shoulderstraps. In 1939 the service color was changed to *Kupferbraun* (copper brown). On April 1, 1943 the *Waffenfarbe* was changed to pink to be used by all reconnaissance units except *Panzeraufklärungabteilung 24*, which retained its original golden yellow pipings.

One of the oldest armored cars in the Wehrmacht inventory was the "Adler" built four-wheeled "Bathtub", shown here in the radio/command version (Kfz.14) on pre-war maneuvers.(BA)

The "Bathtub" in action. As indicated by the all white *Balkenkreuz* national insignia, this photo was taken during the Polish campaign, 1939.(Sch)

During the parade in Vienna after the 1938 *Anschluss*. In the foreground is a Sd.Kfz.247 armored staff car built on the chassis of the "Krupp Prots Kw."(G)

Vienna, 1938. Light four-wheeled armored cars on parade. The vehicles with rectangular engine louvers are Sd.Kfz.221, the others being Sd.Kfz.222s.(G)

An Sd.Kfz.222 light armored car on convoy protection duties during Hitler's visit to the Polish front, 1939.(BA)

The Sd.Kfz.222 was armed with a 20mm gun and a machine gun in a coaxial mounting. This photo was taken during the Polish campaign.(BA)

From 1937 to 1942 a grand total of some 2000 four-wheeled armored cars were built, including all sub-versions. A photo from the Western campaign, 1940.(BA)

A "222" in Paris shortly after the occupation od the French capital by the Germans in 1940.(BA)

The "222" also came with a 28/20mm tapered bore anti-tank gun as main armament in the turret — Tilsit harbor, 1941.(BA)

An older version of the four-wheeled armored car serving with the Waffen-SS 5th SS-Panzer division *Wiking*. This particular vehicle standing alongside a 50mm "Pak 38" anti-tank gun — Eastern front, 1941.(BA)

Concerted action: a cavalry reconnaissance party alongside a reconnaissance car — Russia, 1943.(BA)

Although it was slightly underpowered, the Sd.Kfz.222 was well suited to reconnaissance duties.(BA)

Looking for the enemy. Russian steppe, winter 1941-42.(BA)

In action until the last weeks of the war: a four-wheeled armored car serving with the 19th Panzer Division in Silesia, 1945.(HZ)

Another "222" with the 19th Panzer Division.(HZ)

The bulk of German four-wheeled armored cars used in the Western Desert came equipped with the 20mm main gun in the fully rotating turret.(BA)

Four four-wheeled armored cars are seen here alongside an eight-wheeler.(BA)

Detail of the anti-grenade hinged wire grills upon the comparatively flat open topped turret of the "222."(BA)

A "222" is awaiting transport to Tunisia in front of a six-engined Messerschmitt Me 323 *Gigant* ("Giant") transporter of the Luftwaffe, 1943.(BA)

The radio version of the light four-wheeled armored car standing alongside a *Panzerfunkwagen* vehicle. The letter "K" identifies a vehicle of the 1st Panzer Army.(BA)

An Sd.Kfz.223 in the Western Desert, 1943.(BA)

The standard frame aerial was collapsible mainly for improved all-around fire.(BA)

The first heavy armored car of the Wehrmacht was a six-wheeled vehicle. Here one is shown during pre-war maneuvers.

Parade in Vienna, 1938. A radio armored car 263 alongside a 232 radio vehicle. To the left is an eight-wheeler without rotating turret, to the right is an early version six-wheeler.(G)

An Sd.Kfz.232 six-wheeled armored car on pre-war maneuvers.(Sch)

In action during the Polish campaign. The standard versions of both six- and eight-wheeled armored cars came with the same main armament as the four-wheeled.(BA)

A six-wheeled Sd.Kfz.231 of the 2nd Panzer Division in action during the French campaign, 1940. The rack rigged at the top of the radiator holds smoke canisters to be ignited from the vehicle interior.(BA)

Another view of the six-wheeler. The letter "G" indicating the *Guderian* Panzer Group is shown to advantage. In the background is a "223."(BA)

As late as 1942, this six-wheeler still served as a command car for communication duties in the 6th Panzer Division.(BA)

By 1942 the six-wheelers had been superseded in service by eight-wheeled armored cars. Shown here are troops of the **LAH** in action during the Balkan campaign.(BA)

In the foreground is an eight-wheeler of the 2nd SS-Panzer division *Das Reich*.(BA)

The Western Desert was ideally suited to mobile warfare.(BA)

An eight-wheeled radio armored car of the 3rd Panzer Division with the guyed pole aerial extended. This type of radio equipment had a range of some 200 kilometers.(BA)

Besides the *Panzerfunkwagen* Sd.Kfz.263 there was a *Panzerspähwagen/Fu* radio vehicle, which came equipped with the standard frame aerial and a 20mm gun plus coaxial MG in a fully rotating turret.(BA)

This *Panzerspähwagen/Fu* Sd.Kfz.232 is shown here in action in Greece, 1941.(BA)

An uncommon combination was the tactical sign of motorcycle rifle units positioned on eight-wheeled armored cars as seen here with vehicles of the Panzer-grenadier Division *Grossdeutschland*.(BA)

Western Desert in front of Tobruk. In the background is a German four-wheeled armored car.(BA)

A heavy eight-wheeled armored car Sd.Kfz.233 with 75mm short-barrelled L/24 gun. The non-regulation searchlights of this vehicle are of particular interest.(BA)

Many eight-wheeled armored cars featured additional armored plates on the front for extra protection.(BA)

An action shot from Tunisia. This type of vehicle lacked a rotatable turret.(BA)

In 1943, a refined version of this vehicle was introduced. The chassis was produced by "Büssing-NAG." Officially designated Sd.Kfz.234, this vehicle was externally distinguishable by its single long mudguard on each side.(Sch)

With a 50mm L/60 gun in a fully rotating enclosed turret, this vehicle, the Sd.Kfz.234/2, was known as the *Puma*.(Sch)

With its long 75mm anti-tank gun L/48, the Sd.Kfz.234/4 had good tank hunting capabilities, but was only produced in very limited numbers.(Sch)

The Wehrmacht made extensive use of captured foreign equipment. Here is a French built "Panhard 178" armored car taken over by the Germans from the Czechoslovakian army after their occupation.(BA)

A batch of ex-Czechoslovakian "Panhards", which were used operationally by the Germans during the Western campaign in 1940.(BA)

Captured during the Western campaign, this "panhard" was equipped afterwards with a standard German frame aerial. The extra shield on the front is of particular interest.(BA)

A rail-bound version of the "Panhard" armored car on security duties, 1942.(BA)

A "Panhard" with modified turret to take the standard German 37mm anti-tank gun. These vehicles were mostly used for anti-partisan duties in the hinterland.(BA)

The Austrian "Bundesheer" (Federal Army) had an Austro-Daimler built eight-wheeled armored car. Here some of these vehicles are seen parading in Vienna after the *Anschluss*, 1938.(G)

The Austro-Daimler eight-wheelers were taken over by the Wehrmacht in 1938 and received *Balkenkreuz* national insignias in 1940, in common with all types of German AFVs by this time.(BA)

SUMMARY

Unit	Wehrkreis of origin	Division	Notes
A.A.Lehr	III	H.Tr. 48.V.G.Div. (1944)	aus Kav.Lehr u. Vers. Abt.; wurde 1941 A.A. (mot) 21; später wieder aufgestellt
A.A.GD	III	Inf.Div. (mot) GD	wurde 1943 Pz.A.A. GD
Pz.A.A. FHH	XX	Pz.Gren. Div. FHH	
Pz.A.A.Fü. Begl.Div.	III	Fü.Begl. Div.	bei Fü.Begl.Brig. als Kp. (Pz.Späh Kp.)
Pz.A.A. Brandenburg	III	Pz.Gren. Div. Brandenburg	außerd. Pz.Aufkl.Kp. Fü.Gren.Brig. (Div.)
A.A.(mot)	1	I	1.Kav.Brig. H.Tr. 3.Pz.Div.	wurde A.A.(mot) 118
Pz.A.A.	1	IX	1.Pz.Div.	
A.A.(mot)	2	II	2.Inf.Div. (mot) 12.Pz.Div.	
Pz.A.A.	2	XVII	2.Pz.Div.	
A.A.(mot)	3	III	3.Pz.Div. 5.le.Div. 21.Pz.Div.	
Pz.A.A.	3	III	3.Pz.Div.	
A.A.(mot)	4	IX	1.Pz.Div.	
Pz.A.A.	4	XIII	4.Pz.Div.	
A.A.(mot)	5	XVII	2.Pz.Div.	
Pz.A.A.	5	VIII	5.Pz.Div.	aus Krdschtz.Btl. 24
A.A.(mot)	6	VI	1.le.Div. 6.Pz.Div.	
Pz.A.A.	6	VI	6.Pz.Div.	
A.A.(mot)	7	XIII	4.Pz.Div.	
A.Rgt.(mot)	7	IX	2.le.Div.	wurde A.A.(mot) 37 und Kradschtz.Btl. 7
Pz.A.A.	7	IX	7.Pz.Div.	
A.A.(mot)	8	VIII	5.Pz.Div.	
A.Rgt.(mot)	8	III	10.Pz.Div. 3.le.Div.	I. Abt. II.Abt.; wurde A.A. (mot) 59
A.A.(mot)	9	XVII	9.Pz.Div.	
Pz.A.A.	9	XVII	9.Pz.Div.	
A.A.(mot)	10	XIII	10.Inf.Div. (mot)	
Pz.A.A.	11	VIII	11.Pz.Div.	
Pz.A.A.	12	II	12.Pz.Div.	
A.A.(mot)	13	XI	13.Inf.Div. (mot)	
Pz.A.A.	13	XI	13.Pz.Div.	
A.A.(mot)	14	IV	14.Inf.Div. (mot)	
Pz.A.A.	14	IV	14.Pz.Div.	
Schn.Abt.	15	XII	15.Pz.Gren. Div.	(1943)
Pz.A.A.	16	VI	16.Pz.Div.	auch Schtz.Btl.(gep.) 16 genannt
A.A.(mot)	16	VI	16.Pz.Div.	
Pz.A.A.	17	VII	17.Pz.Div.	
A.A.(mot)	18	VIII	18.Inf.Div. (mot)	in Krdschtz.Btl. 38 aufgeg.
A.A.(mot)	19	XI	19.Pz.Div.	auch Pz.A.A. 19
A.A.(mot)	20	X	20.Inf.Div. (mot)	aus Krdschtz.Btl. 20
Pz.A.A.	20	XI	20.Pz.Div.	
A.A.(mot)	21	VI	21.Pz.Div.	aus A.A. Lehr-(mot)
Pz.A.A.	21	VI	21.Pz.Div.	vh.(Pz.)A.A. 931
A.A.(mot)	22	XII	22.Pz.Div.	vh. A.A.(mot) 140 (?)
Pz.A.A.	23	V	23.Pz.Div.	
A.A.(mot)	24	I	24.Pz.Div.	
Pz.A.A.	24	I	24.Pz.Div.	
A.A.(mot)	25	V	25.Inf.Div. (mot)	
Pz.A.A.	25	VI	25.Pz.Div.	
A.A.(mot)	26	III	26.Pz.Div.	
Pz.A.A.	26	III	26.Pz.Div.	
A.A.(mot)	27	VII	17.Pz.Div.	
A.A.(mot)	29	IX	29.Inf.Div. (mot)	
A.A.(mot)	33	XII	15.Pz.Div.	
A.A.(mot)	36	XII	36.Inf.Div. (mot)	
A.A.(mot)	37	IX	7.Pz.Div.	
A.A.(mot)	40	IV	14.Pz.Div.	1940 aus Teilen A.A. (mot) 4, 7, 8
Schn.Abt.	48	VII	XXII.Geb.K.	
A.A.(mot)	53	III	3.Inf.Div. (mot)	auch Pz.A.A. 53 gen.; s. 103
A.A.(mot)	54	IV	14.Inf.Div.	
A.A.(mot)	55		XV.Kos.Kav. K.	vorh. bei 1.Kos.Kav. Div.
A.A.(mot)	57	VI	6.Pz.Div.	vorh. A.A.(mot) 6
A.A.(mot)	59	III	8.Pz.Div.	
A.A.(mot)	68		Gen.Kdo. z.b.V. LXVIII	
A.A.(mot)	88	IV	18.Pz.Div.	
A.A.(mot)	90	V	10.Pz.Div. 90.le.Afr. Div.	
Pz.A.A.	90		90.Pz.Gren. Div.	(1943)
A.A.(mot)	92	IX	20.Pz.Div.	
Pz.A.A.	103	III	3.Pz.Gren. Div.	aus Pz.A.A. 53
Pz.A.A.	110	XIII	10.Pz.Gren. Div.	aus Krdschtz.Btl. 40
Pz.A.A.	115	XII	15.Pz.Gren. Div.	Aufstellung fraglich
Pz.A.A.	116	VI	16.Pz.Gren. Div., 116.Pz.Div.	aus Krdschtz. Btl. 165

Unit	Wehrkreis of origin	Division	Notes
Pz.A.A.	118	VIII	18.Pz.Gren. Div.
Pz.A.A.	120	X	20.Pz.Gren. Div.
Pz.A.A.	122	X	22.Inf.Div. (LL) vorh. . A.A.(mot.) 122
Pz.A.A.	125	V	25.Pz.Gren. Div.
A.A.(mot.)	128	V	23.Pz.Div.
Pz.A.A.	129	IX	29.Pz.Gren. Div.
Pz.A.A.	130	III/XI	Pz.Lehr Div. aus Pz.A. Lehr A.
A.A.(mot.)	140	XII	22.Pz.Div.
Pz.A.A.	144		Pz.Div. Holstein
A.A.(mot.)	160	XX	60.Inf.Div. (mot.)
Pz.A.A.	160	XX	Pz.Gren. Div. FHH
A.A.(mot.)	165	VI	16.Inf.Div. (mot.) aus Kradschtz.Bt. 165
A.A.(mot.)	168	III	68.Inf.Div. zeitweise
VW-A.Kp.	178	V	78.Sturm Div.
A.A.(mot.)	220	IV	164.le.Afr. Div.
A.A.(mot.)	231	VIII	11.Pz.Div.
A.Zug	188		Sd.Vbd.288 außerdem Pz.Sp.Tr.288
A.A.(mot.)	341	VI	16.Inf.Div. (mot.) 341.Pz.Gren. Div.
A.A.(mot.)	386		386.Pz.Gren. aus Kradschtz.Btl. 386 Div.
A.A.(mot.)	400		H.Tr. zeitw. bei GD(?)
Pz.Sp.Kp. (z.b.V.)	468	III LXVIII	Gen.Kdo. z.b.V. sp. zu A.A.(mot.) 68(?) 6 KWK 7,5 cm, 14 KWK 2 cm
Aufkl.Kp. (mot.)	190		Div. z.b.V. Afrika: 90.le.Div.
A.A.(mot.)	345		345.Pz.Gren. aus Kradschtz.Btl. 345 Div.
gem. Pz.A.A.	520		H.Tr.
A.A.(mot.)	580	III	H.Tr./90.le.Div.
(Pz.)A.A.	931		21.Pz.Div. wird Pz.A.A. 21
Pz.A.A.	999		Sturm Div. Rhodos Bewährungstruppe
A.A.(mot.)	1000		H.Tr. wird Jan. 45 Füs.Btl 716
Pz.A.Kp.	2101		Pz.Brig.101
Pz.A.Kp.	2102		Pz.Brig.102
Pz.A.Kp.	2103		Pz.Brig.103
Pz.A.Kp.	2104		Pz.Brig.104
Pz.A.Kp.	2105	VIII	Pz.Brig.105
Pz.A.Kp.	2106	XX	Pz.Brig.106
Pz.A.Kp.	2107	V	Pz.Brig.107
Pz.A.Kp.	2108	XIII	Pz.Brig.108
Pz.A.Kp.	2109		Pz.Brig.109
Pz.A.Kp.	2110		Pz.Brig.110
Pz.A.Kp.	2111	VI	Pz.Brig.111
Pz.A.Kp.	2112	V	Pz.Brig.112
Pz.A.Kp.	2113	XIII	Pz.Brig.113
Vfg.Kp. Sd.Stab F		III	Sd.Stab F wurde Pz.Sp.Kp. 468

A four-wheeled armored car. Note the steel helmets in front of the searchlights, the ammo boxes on the front and the horseshoe fixed to the fender.(BA)

SUMMARY OF ALL DIVISIONS WITH PANZER-GRENADIER, MOTORCYCLE & PANZER RECONNAISSANCE UNITS ON STRENGTH

By the outbreak of war in 1939, the Wehrmacht had:

    5 Panzer Divisions (1st to 5th)
    4 Light Divisions (1st to 4th) and
    4 Motorized Infantry Divisions (2nd, 13th, 20th and 29th)

on strength. The average established (personal, vehicles and weapons) of each of these divisions was as follows:

	Pz. Div.	L. Div.	Mot. Inf. Div.
Officers	394	332	429
Army officials	115	105	133
NCOs	1,962	1,616	2,456
Other Ranks	9,321	8,716	13,364
Total	11,792	10,772	13,364
Battle tanks	324	86	–
Reconnaissance Vehicles	101	70-131	30
Lorries	1,402	1,368	1,687
Passenger cars	561	595	989
Motorcycles (Solo)	1,289	1,098	1,323
Motorcycles (combinations)	711	606	621
Total	4,388	3,884	4,650
150mm heavy field howitzers	8	–	12
105mm light field howitzers	16	24	36
Cannons	4	–	–
75mm Inf. field howitzers	8	12	12
80mm medium mortars	18	24	24
50mm light mortars	30	42	84
20mm light anti-aircraft guns	12	12	12
Heavy machine guns	46	62	130
Light machine guns (including vehicle mounted)	71	57	15
20mm guns (tank mounted)	71	57	15
37mm guns (tank mounted)	22	11	–
75mm guns (tank mounted)	12	6	–

After the outbreak of war in 1939 reinforcements began to reach these divisions in a steady flow, thus not only their divisional light *Panzer I* AFVs being superseded by more potent *Panzer II* tanks, but also their artillery elements being strengthened by heavy (150mm) "infantry howitzers" and — after 1940 — by heavy 88mm anti-aircraft guns. Besides that there was also a series of reorganizations. As an example, the 11th Panzer Regiment, which had been an independent *Heerestruppen* unit originally, was transferred to 1st Light Division by the outbreak of the war, thus adding to the fighting power of the original panzer element of this division, the *Panzerabteilung 65*, making the 1st Light Division the strongest *de facto* panzer division of the German army. Both the 11th Panzer Regiment and the *Panzerabteilung 65* were by then equipped with the ex-Czechoslovakian *Panzer 35(t)* tank, which was armed with a hard hitting 37mm gun plus two machine guns.

During the war years the organization of all German panzer and panzer-grenadier divisions was reformed several times according to battle-field experiences. As an example, the 1944 order of battle is shown for a panzer and a panzer-grenadier division:

	Pz. Div.	Pz. Gren. Div.
Officers	408	402
Army officials	84	83
NCOs	3,146	2,766
Other Ranks	10,289	11,487
Total	**14,727**	**14,738**
Battle tanks (Mk. IV and Mk. V)	170	3
Reconnaissance Vehicles	16	20
Assault Guns	–	42
Retriever tanks	4	2
Medium APCs	232	7
Light APCs	55	–
Lorries	1,443	1,482
Lorries (fully-tracked or half-tracked vehicles of the *Mule* series)	136	172
Special duty lorries	82	77
Trailers	162	117
Prime movers	125	113
Passenger cars	641	902
Motorcycles (including combinations)	164	153
3/4 tracked *Kettenkräder*	304	322
Total	**3,630**	**3,412**
150mm heavy field howitzers	14	12
150mm heavy infantry guns (how.)	12	8
120mm heavy mortars	18	26
105mm light field howitzers	25	37
100mm cannons	4	4
88mm heavy anti-aircraft guns	12	12
88mm medium mortars	52	64
75mm guns (in vehicle mounts)	106	65
75mm guns (towed)	34	19
50mm anti-tank guns	–	106
37mm anti-tank guns	17	9
20mm guns	47	89
Heavy machine guns	47	89
Light machine guns	1,239	818

As can be seen from the table above, the 1944 personal strength of both panzer and panzer-grenadier divisions was nearly equal, while the vehicle/men ratio had changed considerably by the same time. While a 1944 panzer division statistically had one vehicle per 4.1 men, the respective 1939 ratio had been 1:2.7. The same was true for panzer-grenadier divisions, the 1:3.5 vehicle/men ratio just before the outbreak of war changing to 1:4.3 by 1944. By 1944 the number of battle tanks, reconnaissance vehicles and motorcycles had decreased, while at the same time panzer and panzer-grenadier divisions had several newly introduced AFV, APC and "soft" vehicle types on strength (assault guns, APCs, prime movers, trailers and *Kettenkräder* prime movers). Even in 1944 the infantry elements of some crack divisions (e.g. *Grossdeutschland* and Waffen-SS divisions) only were equipped with APCs, while the bulk of panzer-grenadier divisions still had to make do with wheeled vehicles.

During the later war years the firepower of panzer and panzer-grenadier divisions was steadily increasing due to the increasing number of weapons (especially 75mm guns) per division and to the tendency of introducing larger caliber weapons.

By rebuilding several infantry divisions to panzer (panzer-grenadier) divisions, and by raising new divisions and smaller special units (*GD*, *HG*, and Waffen-SS units) to full divisional status, the Wehrmacht theoretically had:

40 Panzer divisions

5 Light divisions

38 Panzer-grenadier divisions (including motorized infantry divisions) and,

9 Panzer brigades

on strength, making up a grand total of 92 divisional or brigade strength units. In fact this number was not correspondent to reality, as all light divisions and several panzer-grenadier divisions were rebuilt to panzer divisions over the war years. There were also several brigades raised to full divisional status and strength, while in a few cases panzer divisions were reorganized as panzer-grenadier divisions. In fact, the German army (Heer) and the Waffen-SS together had a grand total of 72 large scale motorized or partly armored units (65 divisions and 7 brigades) on strength. To institute and supply all these units despite continuing high losses, the German war industry had to be geared to maximum.

Only 39 out of the above mentioned grand total of 72 large scale units had been instituted by 1941 and soldiered on until the end of the war, while the remainder of these units was either raised in 1942 or later, disbanded or rebuilt to form partly motorized units only.

Battle in the Steppe: While the artillery is shelling a distant target, battle tanks are attacking. In the center dismounted panzer-grenadiers are advancing. The vehicle on the right side is an armored ambulance Sd.Kfz.251/8.(BA)

DIVISIONAL INSIGNIAS

Divisional insignias — sometimes incorrectly referred to as "tactical insignias" — were not instituted before 1940. While at first the use of such signs was restricted to panzer divisions exclusively, after 1941 each division received its distinguishing insignia, which came in white for infantry divisions (marching or motorized), pink for panzer divisions, while mountain divisions were to use green for their divisional insignia. While originally introduced for identification purposes only, these insignias finally gained higher and symbolic importance. The original as well as the 1941 new insignias of the 1st to 18th Panzer Divisions were abstracts designed to a system developed by the OKH (Army High Command), whereby traditions and wishes of the divisions concerned were completely ignored. The 19th Panzer Division was the first unit to adopt a sign corresponding to its own proposals, a new trend, which was to be followed in consequence by all other German divisions as well, the divisional insignias thus getting progressively expressive.

Divisional insignias would normally be painted directly on the standard gray vehicles, on desert yellow vehicles insignias would sometimes be painted on a black rectangular or shield like background. Divisional emblems would sometimes be changed at short notice for enemy deception purposes, an example for this being the 6th Panzer Division, whose traditional "XX" emblem was replaced by a stylized chopper for a short time, when this division was transferred from the Leningrad area to Army Group Center in autumn 1941.

The following table shows all those large scale units, which attained near divisional or brigade strength status, and fought several actions in a more than improvised *ad hoc* battle-group status.

As panzer-grenadier regiments varied in numbers, designation and numerical system over the war years in several cases and motorcycle battalions were no longer in existence after 1943, a key-year is added for each individual unit. Under *Bemerkungen* (remarks) the reader will find described the final fate of each respective division.

Ukraine, 1941 — after the battle. While villages and vehicles are still burning in the background, a battle group prepares for further advance. Shown are Mk.II and Mk.III panzers, and a complement of light and medium APCs.(BA)

DIVISION	DIVISIONAL INSIGNIA	DATE OF FORMATION	PZ.GREN.DIV.* WITHIN THE DIVISION (1943)	MOTORCYCLE (1941) & PZ.RECON. (1943) BATTALIONS WITHIN THE DIVISION	NOTES
			PANZER-GRENADIER DIVISIONS **		
2nd	———	1937	5th 25th 92nd (only in Poland 1939, afterwards 60th Inf.Div.[Mot.])		Reorganized into the 12th Pz.Div. 1940 (see 12th Pz.Div.)
3rd		1940 from 3rd Inf.Div.	8th 29th	53rd (103rd)	The End: 1943 Stalingrad; reorganized
10th		1940 from 10th Inf.Div.	20th 41st	40th (110th)	The End: 1945 on the Weichsel; reorganized afterwards
13th	———	1937	66th 93rd 33rd (only in Poland 1939)		Reorganized as the 13th Pz.Div. during the campaign in France 1940
14th		1940 from 14th Inf.Div.	11th 53rd	54th (114th)	From 1942 on, only semi-motorized
15th		1943 from 15th Pz.Div. over *Sizilien* Div.	104th 115th 129th *Reggio*	15th (Mobile Battalion) (115th)	
16th		1940 from 16th Inf.Div.	60th 156th	165th (116th)	Became 116th Pz.Div. 1944
18th		1940 from 18th Inf. Div.	30th 51st	38th (118th)	

* In divisions that were disbanded or renamed before 1943 (see notes), the regiments were named according to their origins or years of foundation: Schützen-, Kavallerieshützen- or Infantry Regiments (Motorized).

** The designation "Panzer-grenadier Division" existed for Infantry Divisions (Motorized) only as of 1943.

DIVISION	DIVISIONAL INSIGNIA	DATE OF FORMATION	PZ.GREN.DIV. WITHIN THE DIVISION (1943)	MOTORCYCLE (1941) & PZ.RECON. (1943) BATTALIONS WITHIN THE DIVISION	NOTES
20th		1937 from 20th Inf.Div.	76th 90th 69th (only in Poland, 1939)	30th (120th)	69th Reg. went to the 10th Pz.Div.
22nd		1942 from 22nd Inf.Div.	16th 65th	22nd (122nd)	Was equipped and reformed as *Luftlande* Div.
25th		1940 from 25th Inf.Div.	35th 119th	25th (125th)	
29th		1937 from 29th Inf.Div.	15th 71st 86th (only in Poland, 1939)	29th (129th)	End: 1943 in Staling then reformed; 86th Reg. went to 10th Pz.Div.
36th		1940 from 36th Inf.Div.	87th 118th	36th (136th)	Only partly motorized as of 1942
60th		1940	92nd 120th	160th (160th)	End: 1943 in Staling then reformed as Pz.Gren.Div. *Feldherenhalle*
90th		1943 from 90th Lt.Div.	(155th) 200th 361st (T.Mot.)	(580th)	End: 1943 in Africa, the reformed over th *Sardinia* Div.
164th		1943 from 164th Lt.Div.	(125th) 382nd 433rd (440th)	(220th)	End: 1943 in Africa, not reformed.

DIVISION	DIVISIONAL INSIGNIA	DATE OF FORMATION	PZ.GREN.DIV. WITHIN THE DIVISION (1943)	MOTORCYCLE (1941) & PZ.RECON. (1943) BATTALIONS WITHIN THE DIVISION	NOTES
999th	———	1943 Special unit for African Campaign			End: 1943 in Africa, not reformed.
Groß-deutschland (*GD*)	white steel helmet	1942 from the guard unit of the Army Rgt. (1939) and Brig. (1941)	Pz.Gren.Rgt. *GD* (1st Arm.) Pz.Füs..Rgt. *GD* (2nd)	(*GD*)	Was reformed as a Pz.Div. in 1943.
Führer-Grenadier Division (*FGD*)	same as Großdeutschland steel helmet except blue	1945 from *Führer-Grenadier Brigade*	1st *FGD* (Arm.) 2nd *FGD* (Mot.)	(*FGD*)	Was no longer fully formed.
Führer-Begleit Division (*FBD*)	same as Großdeutschland steel helmet except yellow	1945 from *Führer-Begleit Brigade*	1st *FBD* (Arm.) 2nd *FBD* (Mot.)	(*FBD*)	Was no longer fully formed.
Branden-burg (*BR*)	same as Großdeutschland steel helmet except with red Brandenburg eagle	1944 as a Special unit	1st *BR* 2nd*BR* 3rd *BR* 4th *BR*	(*BR*)	
Feldherrnhalle		1943 from the remnants of the 60th Inf.Div. (Mot.)	Pz.Gren.Rgt. *FHH* (1st) Pz.Füs.Rgt. *FHH* (2nd)	(*FHH*)	

PANZER-GRENADIER DIVISIONS OF THE WAFFEN-SS

1st *Leibstandarte Adolf Hitler* (*LAH*)		1941 as Rgt. (1939) and Brigade (1940)	1st (1st *LAH*) 2nd (2nd *LAH*)	*LAH*	Was reformed as a Pz.Div. in 1942 (see there).

DIVISION	DIVISIONAL INSIGNIA	DATE OF FORMATION	PZ.GREN.DIV. WITHIN THE DIVISION (1943)	MOTORCYCLE (1941) & PZ.RECON. (1943) BATTALIONS WITHIN THE DIVISION	NOTES
2nd *Das Reich*	(insignia)	1941 from SS-Verf. Div. (Mot.) (since 1939)	3rd *Deutschland* 4th *Der Führer*		Was reformed as a Pz.Div. 1942 (see there).
3rd *Totenkopf*	(insignia)	1940	5th *Thule* 6th *Theodor Eicke*		Was reformed as a Pz.Div. 1942 (see there).
4th *Polizei-Division*	(insignia)	1942 from *Ordnungstruppen der Polizei* (1939) (1942 Mot.)	7th 8th	4th	
5th *Wiking*	(insignia)	1941	9th *Germania* 10th *Westland*	5th	Consisted of volunteers from north and west European countries; was reformed as a Pz.Div. in 1943 (see there).
9th *Hohenstaufen*	(insignia)	1943	19th 20th	9th	Was reformed as a Pz.Div. in 1944 (see there).
10th *Karl der Große*	——	1943	21st 22nd	10th	Was later reorganized in 1943 as the *Frundsberg* Pz.Div. (see there).
11th *Nordland*	(insignia)	1943	23rd *Norge* 24th *Danmark*	11th	Consisted of volunteers from Nordic countries; was later reorganized as a Pz.Div. in 1943 (see there).
16th *Reichführer SS (RFSS)*		1944 from *Sturmberigade RFSS* (1943)	35th 36th	16th	

DIVISION	DIVISIONAL INSIGNIA	DATE OF FORMATION	PZ.GREN.DIV. WITHIN THE DIVISION (1943)	MOTORCYCLE (1941) & PZ.RECON. (1943) BATTALIONS WITHIN THE DIVISION	NOTES
17th *Götz von Berlichingen*		1943	37th 38th	(17th)	
18th *Horst Wessel*		1944	39th 40th	(18th)	In some cases the *SA* emblem was used as the divisional emblem.
23rd *Nederland*		1944	(48th) *General Seyffardt* (49th) *De Ruyter*	(54th)	Composed of volunteers from the Netherlands; only reached brigade strength.
26th *Ungarn* (Nr.3)	——	1945	64th 65th	(26th)	Composed of volunteers from Hungary; only reached brigade strength.
27th *Langemark*		1944	66th (67th) *Langemark* 68th	(27th)	Composed of Flemish volunteers; only reached brigade strength.
28th *Wallonien*		1945	(69th) *Wallonie* 70th	(28th)	Composed of Walloon volunteers; only reached brigade strength.
38th *Nibelungen*		1945	95th 96th 97th	(38th)	Only reached brigade strength.
Fallschirm- Pz.Gren.Div. 2 *Hermann Göring*		1944 (reorganized)	3rd *HG* (Mot.) 4th *HG* (Mot.)	— (2nd *HG*)	

DIVISION	DIVISIONAL INSIGNIA	DATE OF FORMATION	PZ.GREN.DIV. WITHIN THE DIVISION (1943)	MOTORCYCLE (1941) & PZ.RECON. (1943) BATTALIONS WITHIN THE DIVISION	NOTES
			LIGHT DIVISIONS*		
1st	–	1938	4th (1939)	6th	Became 6th Pz.Div. 1939/40
2nd	–	1938	6th (1939) 7th (1939)	–	Became 7th Pz.Div. 1939/40
3rd	–	1938	8th (1939) 9th (1939)	8th	Became 8th Pz.Div. 1939/40
4th	–	1938	10th (1939) 11th (1939)	–	Became 9th Pz.Div. 1939/40
5th	Palm tree in coat-of-arms Shield	1941	200th (with the 2nd MG-Btl.)	–	Was established as a blockade unit for Africa and reformed there as the 21st Pz.Div. in 1941/42.
			PANZER DIVISIONS		
1st	(1940) (1941)	1935	1st (Mot.) 113th (Arm.)	1st (1st)	
2nd	(1940) (1941)	1935	2nd (Mot.) 304 (Arm.)	2nd (2nd)	after 1943

* Not to be confused with the Light Infantry Divisions, established later and usually given higher numbers, they were not motorized and were a mixture of infantry and mountain divisions. They were intended for combat in terrain with few roads and not motorized. The divisions listed here were fully motorized from the beginning, but in terms of numbers weaker and more easily mobile than Panzer Divisions.

DIVISION	DIVISIONAL INSIGNIA		DATE OF FORMATION	PZ.GREN.DIV. WITHIN THE DIVISION (1943)	MOTORCYCLE (1941) & PZ.RECON. (1943) BATTALIONS WITHIN THE DIVISION	NOTES
3rd	(1940)	(1941)	1935	3rd (Arm.) 394th (Mot.)	3rd (3rd)	
4th	(1940)	(1941)	1938	12th (Arm.) 33rd (Mot.)	34th 94th)	
5th	(1940)	(1941)	1938	13th (Mot.) 14th (Arm.)	55th (5th)	
6th	(1940)	(1941)	1939/40 from 1st Lt. Div.	4th (Mot.) 114th (Arm.)	6th (6th)	
7th	(1940)	(1941)	1939/40 from 2nd Lt.Div.	6th (Arm.) 7th (Mot.)	7th (7th)	
8th	(1940)	(1941)	1939/40 from 3rd Lt.Div.	8th (Mot.) 28th (Mot.)	8th (8th)	
9th	(1940)	(1941)	1939/40 from 4th Lt.Div.	10th (mot.) 11th (Arm.)	59th (9th)	

167

DIVISION	DIVISIONAL INSIGNIA	DATE OF FORMATION	PZ.GREN.DIV. WITHIN THE DIVISION (1943)	MOTORCYCLE (1941) & PZ.RECON. (1943) BATTALIONS WITHIN THE DIVISION	NOTES
10th	Y··· (1940) Y‖‖ (1941)	1939 from 4th Pz.Brig.	69th (Arm.) 86th (Mot.)	10th (10th)	End: Tunis 1943 afterwards no new reorganization
11th	⊖	1940 from 11th Schütz.Brig.	110th (Arm.) 11th (Mot.)	61st (11th)	Special Insignia
12th	⊖	1940 from 2nd Inf.Div. (Mot.)	5th (Mot.) 25th (Mot.)	22nd (12th)	
13th	⊕	1940 from 13th Inf.Div. (Mot.)	66th (Arm.) 93rd (Mot.)	43rd (13th)	Was reformed in 19. as the *Feldher-rnhalle* Pz.Div. End: 1945 in Budapest.
14th	⧫	1940 from 4th Inf.Div.	103rd (Arm.) 108th (Mot.)	64th (14th)	End: 1943 in Stalingrad, not reformed.
15th	⊿	1940 from 33rd Inf.Div.	104th (Arm.) 115th (Mot.)	15th (33rd)	End 1943 in Tunis, later reformed as Pz.Gren.Div.
16th	⚥	1940 from 16th Inf.Div.	64th (Arm.) 79th (Mot.)	16th (16th)	End: 1943 in Stalingrad, later reformed.

DIVISION	DIVISIONAL INSIGNIA	DATE OF FORMATION	PZ.GREN.DIV. WITHIN THE DIVISION (1943)	MOTORCYCLE (1941) & PZ.RECON. (1943) BATTALIONS WITHIN THE DIVISION	NOTES
17th		1940 from 27th Inf.Div.	40th (Mot.) 63rd (Mot.)	17th (17th)	
18th		1940 from 4th Unit 14th Inf.Div.	52nd (Mot.) 101st (Mot.)	18th (18th)	Reformed as an artillery Div. 1943.
19th		1940 from 19th Inf.Div.	73rd (Mot.) 74th (Arm.)	19th (19th)	
20th	from 1942	1940 from 19th Inf.Div.	59th (Mot.) 112th (Mot.)	20th (20th)	
21st	from 1942	1941 from 5th Lt.Div.	125th (Arm.) 192nd (Arm.)	– (21st)	End: 1943 in Tunis; reformed in 1944, originally as occupation troops in France.
22nd		1941	129th 140th	24th (140th)	Disbanded after its first combat actions in 1943.
23rd	Special Insignia	1941	126th (Arm.) 128th (Mot.)	23rd (23rd)	
24th	from 1944	1942 from 1st Cav.Div.	21st (Mot.) 26th (Arm.)	4th (24th)	End: 1943 in Stalingrad later reformed.

169

DIVISION	DIVISIONAL INSIGNIA	DATE OF FORMATION	PZ.GREN.DIV. WITHIN THE DIVISION (1943)	MOTORCYCLE (1941) & PZ.RECON. (1943) BATTALIONS WITHIN THE DIVISION	NOTES
25th		1942 from *Norwegian* Occupation Units	146th (Arm.) 147th (Mot.)	– (25th)	
26th		1942 from 23rd Inf.Div.	9th (Arm.) 67th (Mot.)	– (26th)	
116th		1944 from 16th Pz.Gren. Division	60th (Arm.) 156th (Mot.)	– (116th)	
Groß- deutschland		1943 from Pz.Gren.Div. *Großdeutschland*	Pz.Gren.Rgt. (1st) *GD* (Arm.) Pz.Fuus.Rgt. *GD* (2nd) (Arm.)	(*GD*) (*G.D.*)	
Panzer- Lehr Division		1943 from *Lehr* troops of the Panzer Units	901st (Arm.) 902nd (Arm.)	(130th)	
1st Pallschirm- Pz.Div. *Hermann Göring*		1943 from *Hermann Göring* Pz.Div.	1st *HG* (Arm.) 2nd *HG* (Arm.)	– (1st *HG*)	
Kurmark	red shield with a red Brrandenburg eagle	1945 from *Ersatztruppen-tielen* *Großdeutschland*		(*Kurmark*)	Established only at Brigade strength
Clausewitz		1945 from *Ersatztruppen- tielen*		(*Clausewitz*)	Established only at Brigade strength

DIVISION	DIVISIONAL INSIGNIA	DATE OF FORMATION	PZ.GREN.DIV. WITHIN THE DIVISION (1943)	MOTORCYCLE (1941) & PZ.RECON. (1943) BATTALIONS WITHIN THE DIVISION	NOTES
1st *Leibstandarte Adolf Hitler* (*LAH*)		1941 Rgt. (1939) Brigade (1940)	1st (*LAH*-1) 2nd (*LAH*-2)	*LAH*	Was reorganized in 1942 as a Pz.Div. (see there).
2nd *Das Reich*		1941 from SS-Veref.Div. (Mot.) (since 1939)	3rd *Deutschland* 4th *Der Führer*		Was reorganized in 1942 as a Pz.Div. (see there).
3rd *Totenkopf*		1940	5th *Thule* 6th *Theodor Eicke*		Was reorganized in 1942 as a Pz.Div. (see there).
5th *Wiking*		1941	9th *Germania* 10th *Westland*	5th	Composed of volunteers from north and west European countries; was reformed in 1943 as a PzDiv. (see there).
9th *Hohenstaufen*		1943	19th 20th	9th	Was reformed in 1944 as a Pz.Div. (see there).
10th *Frundsberg*		1943 From SS-Pz.Gren.Div. Frundsberg	21st (Arm.) 22nd (Arm.)	10th	
11th *Nordland*		1943 from SS-Pz.Gren.Div.	23rd *Norge* (Arm.) 24th *Danmark* (Arm.)	11th	
12th *Hitlerjugend*		1943 formed from the *LAH*	25th (Arm.) 26th (Arm.)	22nd (12th)	

This symbol was also used.

171

PANZER (GRENADIER) BRIGADES*

Führer- Grenadier- Brig. (FGB)	–	1943	FG FB	–	1945 changed to Panzer-Grenadier Division **FGD**
Führer- Begleit- Brig. (FBB)	–	1944	FB	–	1945 changed to Panzer-Grenadier Division **FBD**
103	–	1944	2103	–	
106	–	1944	2106	–	Combined 1945 into Pz.Div. **Feldherrnhalle** (13th Pz. Div.)
107	–	1944	207	–	Combined 1945 into 25th Pz.Gren.Div.
111	–	1944	2111	–	Combined into 11th Pz.Div.
112	–	1944	2112	–	
113	–	1944	2113	–	
150	–	1944	–	–	Special Unit in the Ardennes Offensive

* In the summer of 1944 the establishment of 13 Panzer brigades and one special Panzer brigade was ordered. Only those listed here saw combat action; all the others, without exception, were utilized even before completion to refresh hard-hit Panzer divisions. Their structures were different because some of them included more than just one Panzer-grenadier battalion. These were at times called Panzer-grenadier brigades.

EPILOGUE

Panzer-grenadier, Kradschützen and *Panzer-ufklärer* were new arms of service first introduced into military history by the Germans as direct consequence of General Guderian's revolutionary concept, which made the panzer the central and most important weapon on the battlefield.

As the panzer-grenadiers had to accompany the panzers into battle and fight alongside them in concerted action, it would have been necessary to give armored transport/fighting vehicles also to the grenadiers. This, in fact, the Germans were never able to do during World War II, and even today it will probably not be possible for any war waging nation to equip its infantry masses with APCs. During World War II not even the divisional infantry elements of German panzer divisions could be completely equipped with APCs, let alone the panzer-grenadier divisions, or even elite units like the *Grossdeutschland* division or the divisions of the Waffen-SS. As a rule, only one of the four panzer-grenadier battalions (organized into two regiments) of an average panzer division was equipped with APCs. This armored panzer-grenadier battalion together with the divisional battle tanks acted as a "mailed fist" in action, while the remainder of the divisional grenadier units cooperated with assault guns or tank hunting vehicles in the traditional infantry role.

When in the latter half of World War II enemy anti-tank defenses became even stronger and increasingly powerful, the losses of even armored German infantry rose so dramatically that there were requests for stronger armored APCs. The thinly armored APCs could not longer afford following the panzers into action without risking heavy losses, things getting worse by the growing tendency for panzer-grenadiers not to fight dismounted, but to stay in their APCs which provided them protection against infantry fire and shell splinters at least. So the APCs finally turned into thinly armored and over-crowded "battle tanks", which could not be used any longer in main battles. Retrospectively seen, the parallel development of medium and light APCs must be judged a failure. Economically, it would have been better to equip panzer-grenadier units with medium APCs, once the heyday of the motorcycle on the battlefield was over, while the development of a light APC for the grenadier elements of *Panzeraufklärer* units was a costly extravagance the German war industry could ill afford.

The *Panzeraufklärer* arm was obsessed by its concept of "Reconnaissance in force", which on one hand led to the equipment of reconnaissance forces with infantry elements of their own and with armored vehicles, but on the other hand led to heavy losses and early attrition on battle duties, for which the *Panzeraufklärer* were neither suitably equipped nor trained. Had German reconnaissance units been restricted to their classical role of "seeing, hearing and reporting" only, they would have needed only a handful of small, agile and lightly armored vehicles. But the Germans decided not to follow tried and proven foreign concepts in this particular respect, and formed large scale reconnaissance units up to brigade strength and providing such units heavy six- and eight-wheeled armored cars, tracked vehicles and heavy weapons up to 75mm caliber. Abuses of reconnaissance forces were the result of this concept, an abuse, which we can see nowadays even clearer with the advent of highly sophisticated air reconnaissance and even "drones."

Panzer-grenadiers, motorcycle and panzer reconnaissance units had their common origin in the development of a "motorized fighting arm" (*Kraftfahrkampftruppe*), but the further development of these arms was nor coordinated in the correct way. This led to costly technical and tactical failures for which the Wehrmacht was to pay dearly, especially during the later war years. many of the technical and tactical questions raised then, are even unsettled today, albeit one statement is definitive: *"Kradschützen" have gone once and forever.*

Despite some fair criticism it should never be forgotten that motorcycle, panzer reconnaissance and panzer-grenadier units were unique arms and that they had a definite edge over their enemies during the early phases of World War II. From 1939-1941 they closely cooperated with the panzers and the dive bomber of the Luftwaffe, and thus made decisive contributions to the early crushing "Blitzkrieg" victories of the Wehrmacht. The turn of the tide came during the winter of 1941-42. By autumn 1942 the days of headlong advances were finally over, panzergrenadier and motorcycle rifle units began to suffer heavily in mainly defensive actions, the *Kradschützen* were disbanded as a separate branch of service, and the *Panzeraufklärer* were badly mauled especially during the chronic crises of the later war years.

Together with their comrades of the regular marching infantry, the three arms of service described in this book always had to carry the burden of constantly heavy action. Serving "fire brigade" duties, these units were always engaged at the focal points of the battlefronts, leading a restless life and, since 1943 at least, knowing neither rest nor recreation. Their last desperate actions they even had to fight without their specialized equipment.

The names of all of these units stand for unrivalled heroism as well as for suffering and death.

Undoubtedly, those who let loose World War II must be judged criminals. Never before in history has an army and a whole nation been so totally deceived and abused as during the years of the Nazi regime in Germany. But to judge millions of field gray uniformed men, who fought this war, criminals *en bloc*, would be unfair. It was a crime to start this war, but only a few of those, who were to fight it out really knew what was going on then. They all did their duty — and not only according to their oath of allegiance, as is so often claimed today — but because they believed to serve a just cause.

—

It is beyond the scope of this book to ask or answer the question if "there was any sense in it", this being a political rather than military matter. This question may be justified, but in common with many retrospective contemplations it is put too simply. Thoughts and actions should always be judged from the then contemporary point of view and never retrospectively.

However, one may value soldierly action, it should never be forgotten that these men generously risked and gave their lives for their nation and their families. Thus this book is dedicated to the battles, the achievements and to the soldierly ethos of the panzer-grenadiers, motorcycle and panzer reconnaissance men of the former German Wehrmacht of World War II.

Panzer-grenadier and panzer: they formed an inseparable fighting entity.(HE)

The motorcycle rifle battalion of the Panzer-grenadier Division *Grossdeutschland* is seen here advancing in a wide variety of vehicles. Motorcycles were used for reconnaissance and dispatch duties exclusively.(BA)

SCHIFFER MILITARY HISTORY

Specializing in the German Military of World War II

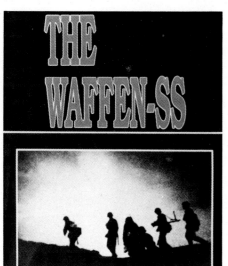

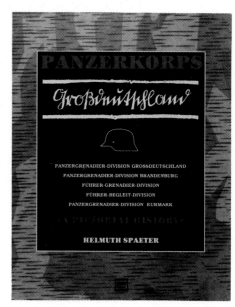